E-1 Treaty Trader Petition

ATTORNEY BRIAN D. LERNER

Law Offices of Brian D. Lerner, A Professional Corporation

Attorney Brian D. Lerner

E-1 Treaty Trader Petition

E-1 Treaty Trader Petition

Print ISBN: 978-1-948774-71-0
Ebook ISBN: 978-1-948774-69-7

INTRODUCTION

There are a multitude of different immigration petitions and applications. They are complex and full of requirements. Obviously it would be best to hire and immigration attorney to best prepare the petitions and application. However, this can certainly cost thousands of dollars.

The next best option is to get a sample of the petition written by an experienced immigration attorney. The samples cost a fraction what would be charged by an immigration attorney. However, while the reader has to alter, amend and change the parts of the sample petition to reflect their actual situation, it is a fantastic roadmap for them to use. If the reader has purchased the entire petition or application, they will have real live samples of cover letters, forms, declarations, affidavits and the necessary exhibits to use. The samples come from real cases and the names of those clients have been redacted to protect the privacy of that person or corporation.

These are petitions and applications that have been drafted by an experienced immigration attorney with over 25 years of experience. Get the benefits of that experience without the costs.

ABOUT THE LAW OFFICES OF BRIAN D. LERNER

The Law Offices of Brian D. Lerner, APC. The law practice consists of Immigration and Nationality Law and everything involved with and regarding immigration which includes citizenship, investment visas, family and employment visas, removal and deportation hearings, appeals, waivers, adjustment, consulate processing and all types of immigration and citizenship matters. Thousands of families have been reunited and/or permitted to stay in the U.S. and/or return to the U.S. because of the successful work of Immigration Attorney Brian D. Lerner.

This law office handles all types of immigration cases including family based and employment based. Immigration issues range from immigration court proceedings to trying to fix what paralegals may have done that was neither correct nor proper. Foreign nationals must have experienced lawyers admitted to practice law.

The Law Offices of Brian D. Lerner, APC handles cases arising from business visas, work permits, Green Cards, non-immigrant visas, deportaion, citizenship, appeals and all areas of immigration. The Law Offices of Brian D. Lerner, APC does EB-5 Investor Visas, H-1B Specialty Occupation, L-1 Intracompany Transferee, E-2 Treaty Investor, E-1 Treaty Trader, O-1 Extraordinary Ability among others. Regarding immigrant visas for the Green Card, the firm does PERM and advanced degree PERM, Family Petitions, and Extraordinary Alien Petitions. In addition to affirmative petitions, the Law Firm represents people in people in deportation and removal hearings, including political asylum, withholding of removal, and convention against torture cases.

Brian D. Lerner has been certified as an expert in Immigration & Nationality Law by the California State Bar, Board of Legal Specialization since 2000 and has been recertified three times. He now passes on his decades of experience by allowing the Reader, Law Schools, Professors and other Immigration Attorneys to purchase sample petitions on every facet of Immigration Law.

TABLE OF CONTENTS

ABOUT THE E-1

Are you an entrepreneur? Want expand your current business into the U.S. and trade with the U.S.? Don't have $1,000,000 for the EB-5? Don't have $100,000 for an E-2 Treaty Investor? If you have already been trading with the U.S., then the E-1 Treaty Trader Visa may be the best option for you. The amount of the investment is much less important and you can come to the U.S. to pursue your dreams. Assuming your from a treaty country, the E-1 Treaty Trader Visa gives you everything you need for the best chance for approval. It includes all relevant cover letters, forms, exhibits, business plan, and supporting evidence. It has been prepared by an expert Immigration attorney. Thus this book will allow you to see a guide of how its done, prepared and submitted.

ATTORNEY COVER LETTER

LAW OFFICES OF
BRIAN D. LERNER
A PROFESSIONAL CORPORATION

BRIAN D. LERNER, ESQ.
CERTIFIED SPECIALIST IN IMMIGRATION AND NATIONALITY LAW

WWW.CALIFORNIAIMMIGRATION.US

ADMITTED TO THE UNITED STATES SUPREME COURT
ADMITTED TO THE U.S. COURTS OF APPEALS FOR THE 1ST THROUGH 11TH CIRCUITS

3233 EAST BROADWAY . LONG BEACH, CALIFORNIA 90803 . TELEPHONE (562) 495-0554 . FACSIMILE (562) 608-8672

September 3, 2015

U.S. Consulate General Melbourne
553 St. Kilda Road
Melbourne, VIC 3004

Re: E-1 Treaty Trader (Employee/Essential Skills)
Petitioner: [redacted] Inc. dba TAS America
Beneficiary/Applicant: [redacted]

Dear Officer:

We respectfully submit the following on behalf of Mr. [redacted] in support of his application for an E-1 Treaty Trader visa an an employee who possesses skills essential to the operations of TAS America, a California corporation, which imports screen printing machinery and parts from TAS International, a registered company in Australia, sells and services TAS International screen printing machines and products in the United States.

<u>Tab</u> <u>Description:</u>

B *Forms*

- DS-160 Confirmation Page
- Form DS-156E
- Visa Fee Receipt
- Form G-28 – TAS America
- Job Letter

C *Applicant Information*

- Passport (Bia Data Page), I-94s and Visa
- Resume or Curriculum Vitae

- Letter of Intent to Depart

D *Ownership*

- Articles of Incorporation
- Fictitious Name Statement
- Share Certificate

E *Trade*

- 2014 International Trade Spreadsheet
- 2014 Invoices
- 2014 Air Bills or Shipping Invoices
- 2015 International Trade Spreadsheet
- 2015 Invoices
- 2015 Air Bills or Shipping Invoices
- 2013 Income Tax Return
- 2014 Income Tax Extension

E-1 TREATY TRADER OR INVESTOR

A nonimmigrant under section 101(a)(15)(E) of the Immigration and Nationality Act (hereinafter "Act"), 8 U.S.C. § 1101(a)(15)(E), is defined as:

> an alien entitled to enter the United States under and in pursuance of the provisions of a treaty of commerce and navigation between the United States and the foreign state of which he is a national, and the spouse and children of any such alien if accompanying or following to join him:
>
> (i) solely to carry on substantial trade, including trade in services or trade in technology, principally between the United States and the foreign state of which he is a national; _
>
> (ii) solely to develop and direct the operations of an enterprise in which he has invested, or of an enterprise in which he is actively in the process of investing, a substantial amount of capital; or
>
> (iii) solely to perform services in a specialty occupation in the United

the Secretary of Homeland Security and the Secretary of State that the intending employer has filed with the Secretary of Labor an attestation under section 212(t)(1).

See also 8 C.F.R. § 214.2(e); 9 FAM § 41.51.

A. ██████ IS A CITIZEN AND NATIONAL OF A TREATY COUNTRY.

The Immigration and Nationality Act (hereinafter "INA" or "Act") requires the existence of a treaty of Friendship, Commerce, and Navigation (hereinafter "FCN") between the United States and another state in order for E visa classification to be accorded to nationals of that state. See INA § 101(a)(15)(E); 9 FAM § 41.51, note 3. As a substitute for a qualifying treaty, legislation has been enacted in certain areas to extend the privilege of the treaty visa status to nationals of certain countries. See 9 FAM § 41.51, note 3.

Australia is a treaty country for the purposes of E-1 classification. See 9 FAM § 41.51, Exhibit I. Mr. ███ is a citizen and national of Australia. **See Tab C, Passport (Bia Data Page), I-94s and Visa.** Therefore, Mr. ███ is a citizen and national of a treaty country.

B. TAS AMERICA'S ACTIVITIES CONSTITUTE TRADE WITHIN THE MEANING OF INA § 101(a)(15)(E).

For E-1 purposes, trade must constitute an exchange, must be international in scope and must involve qualifying activities. See 9 FAM § 41.51, note 4.1-4.5.

In the present case, TAS America is a California corporation which imports screen printing machinery and parts from TAS International, a registered company in Australia, and sells and services TAS International screen printing machines and products in the United States. **See Tab B, Job Letter; and D-E.** Therefore, TAS America's activities constitute trade within the meaning of INA § 101(a)(15)(E).

C. TAS AMERICA'S TRADE WITH TAS INTERNATIONAL IS SUBSTANTIAL.

The word "substantial" is intended to describe the flow of the goods or services that are being exchanged between the treaty countries. The trade must be a continuous flow that should involve numerous transactions over time. Although the number of transactions and the value of each transaction will vary, greater weight should be accorded to cases involving more numerous transactions of larger value. However, smaller businesses should not be excluded if demonstrating a pattern of transactions of value. Thus, proof of numerous transactions, although each ███ be relatively small in value, might establish the requisite continuing course of international trade. See 9 FAM § 41.51, note 6.

In the present, the attached documents establish 21 transactions totaling over $500,000 for 2014 and for the year-to-date, 14 transactions totaling over $300,000. **See Tab E.** Therefore, TAS America's trade with TAS International is substantial.

D. TAS AMERICA'S INTERNATIONAL TRADE IS ENTIRELY BEWEEN THE UNITED STATES AND A TREATY COUNTRY.

The general rule requires that over 50 percent of the total volume of the international trade conducted by the treaty trader regardless of location must be between the United States and the treaty country of the alien's nationality. See 9 FAM § 41.51, note 7.

As evidenced by the attached documents, TAS America's international trade is entirely between the United States and Australia, a treaty country. **See Tab E.**

E. MR. ███ POSSESSES SKILLS ESSENTIAL TO TAS AMERICA'S OPERATIONS IN THE UNITED STATES.

The regulations provide E visa classification for employees who have special qualifications that make the service to be rendered essential to the efficient operation of the enterprise. The employee must, therefore, possess specialized skills and, similarly, such skills must be needed by the enterprise. The determination of whether an employee is an "essential employee" in this context requires the exercise of judgment. It can not be decided by the mechanical application of a bright-line test. By its very nature, essentiality must be assessed on the particular facts in each case. See 9 FAM § 41.51, note 14.3.

In assessing the specialized skills and their essentiality, the following factors should be considered: (1) Degree of proven expertise of the alien in the area of specialization; (2) The uniqueness of the specific skills; (3) The function of the job to which the alien is destined; and (4) The salary such special expertise can command. See 9 FAM § 41.51, note 14.3-2.

In the present case, TAS America is a California corporation which imports screen printing machinery and parts from TAS International, a registered company in Australia, and sells and services TAS International screen printing machines and products in the United States. In turn, Mr. ███ was literally born into a silk screening family and has over 8 years of experience with TAS International machines and products and 4 years of training on TAS International equipment. As TAS America is engaged in the import, sale and service of TAS International machine and products, Mr. ███ experience and expertise is essential to TAS America's operations and something that cannot be found in the U.S. workforce. Furthermore, Mr. ███ PLC (Programmable Logic Controller) and HMI (Human-Machine Interface) programming experience will allow TSA America to adapt this technology and update over 1,000 machines in the Los Angeles area alone. **See Tab B, Job Letter; and Tab C, Resume or Curriculum Vitae.**

Thus, Mr. ███ possesses skills essential to TAS America's operations in the United States.

F. MR. ███ INTENDS TO DEPART THE UNITED STATES UPON TERMINATION OF HIS E-2 STATUS.

An E-2 applicant need not establish his or her intent to proceed to the United States for a specific temporary period of time. See 9 FAM § 41.51, note 15. Nor does an E-2 applicant need to have a residence in a foreign country which the applicant does not intend to abandon. *Id.* Generally, an

In the present case, Mr. ███ intends to depart the United States and return to Australia upon the termination of his E-2 status. **See Tab C, Letter of Intent to Depart.**

CONCLUSION

For the forgoing reasons, Mr. ███ through undersigned counsel, respectfully requests that he be granted an E-1 visa for the maximum initial period.

███

Attorney at Law

FORMS

DS-160 Confirmation Page

U.S. DEPARTMENT of STATE
CONSULAR ELECTRONIC APPLICATION CENTER

Online Nonimmigrant Visa Application (DS-160)

Confirmation

AA005A1812

This confirms the submission of the Nonimmigrant visa application for:

Name Provided:	
Date Of Birth:	
Place of Birth:	
Gender:	Male
Country/Region of Origin (Nationality) :	
Passport Number:	N5338619
Purpose of Travel:	TREATY TRADER (E1)
Completed On:	26 AUG 2015
Confirmation No:	2

Location Selected:

MLB

Australia

Version 01.02.01

THIS IS NOT A VISA

Note: Electronically submitting your DS-160 online application is the FIRST STEP in the visa application process. The next step is to review the internet page of the embassy or consulate where you plan to apply for your visa. Most visa applicants will need to schedule a visa interview, though some applicants qualify for visa renewal. The embassy or consulate information include specific local instructions about scheduling interviews, submitting your visa application, and other frequently asked questions.

YOU MUST BRING the confirmation page and the following document(s) with you at all steps during the application process:

Passport; Evidence of Status or Investment; Employment Contract

You also provide any additional documents you feel will support your case.

FORM
DS-156E

U.S. Department of State

NONIMMIGRANT TREATY TRADER/INVESTOR APPLICATION

USE WITH FORM DS-156/I-129

(USE ADDITIONAL SHEETS OF PAPER, AS NECESSARY, TO COMPLETE RESPONSES)

(See Instruction Page)

PART I - BUSINESS PROFILE

1. Name of U.S. Enterprise, Business, or Company **May National Inc. dba TAS America**

2. Type of Business Enterprise:

[X] Corporation Privately owned [ ] Branch/Liaison Office [ ] Joint Venture [ ] Partnership [ ] Subsidiary [ ] Other

3. Address of Headquarters, Subsidiaries and Branch Offices of U.S. Enterprise *(Specify type of office)*

Telephone Number FAX Number: **N/A**

4. Date *(mm-dd-yyyy)* and Place ...ess Was Established or Incorporated in the United States *(Attach appropriate documentation; e.g., corporate papers, partnership agreement, etc.)*

02/13/2019 California

5. What is the nature of the business?

[ ] General Trade [X] Imports to U.S. [ ] Exports from U.S. [ ] Manufacturing [X] Retail Sales [X] Services/Technology [ ] Other *(Describe)*

6. Describe fully the services, production, or other activity in No. 5 above.

Import of screen printing machinery and parts from TAS International, a registered company in Australia and sales and servicing of TAS International screen printing machines and products in the United States.

7. Name and Address of Foreign Parent Business *(If any)*

N/A

Telephone Number: **N/A** FAX Number: **N/A**

8. Nationality of Foreign Entity *(Corporation, Partnership, etc.)* or Foreign Individual Owner of U.S. Business *(Attach documentation)*

NAME	NATIONALITY	IF INDIVIDUAL INVESTOR, IMMIGRATION STATUS	PERCENT OF OWNERSHIP
	Australian	**E-1**	**100%**
			Total - 100%

9. Financial Statement for year 2014 [X] Calendar Year [ ] Fiscal Year *(Attach most recent financial statement or auditor's report)*

Total Assets of U.S. Business:	496,480.51	[ ] Current Cash	[ ] Historical Cost
Total Liabilities:	319,860.53		
Owner's Equity:*	176,619.98		
Total Annual Operating Income:	475,854	33,599	
	Before Taxes	After Taxes	

* Owner's equity of a corporation refers to paid-in capital plus retained earnings; partner's capital accounts in a partnership; and owner's capital account in a sole proprietorship.

10. To measure the amount of international trade with the United States, please complete the following. *(For trade in merchandise, exports and imports, refer to shipment and sale of goods across international boundaries. For trade in services and technology, exports and imports, refer to the sale of services by treaty-country nationals to nationals of the United States and other countries.)*

Gross International Trade of the U.S. Enterprise in 2014 (year) [X] Calendar Year [ ] Fiscal Year Ending ______

	DOLLAR VALUE	NO. OF TRANSACTIONS (Optional)	PERCENT OF TOTAL TRADE
Imports from treaty country to U.S. business	534,732	21	100
Exports from U.S. business to treaty country	0	0	0
Imports from third countries to U.S. business	0	0	0
Exports from United States to third countries	0	0	0
Domestic U.S. production/manufacturing	0	0	0
Total:	534,732	21	100%

11. Type of Investment *(Check one)*

[ ] Creation of a new business Total Start-up Costs: N/A [ ] Purchase of an existing business Purchase Price: N/A [ ] Continuation of an existing business Fair Market Value of Business: N/A

12. Total Investment from Abroad Made in the United States *(Attach documentation)*

FOR YEAR N/A [ ] Calendar [ ] Fiscal

	INITIAL INVESTMENT	TOTAL CUMULATIVE INVESTMENT
Cash	N/A	N/A
Inventory	N/A	N/A
Equipment	N/A	N/A
Premises	N/A	N/A
Other *(describe)*	N/A	N/A
TOTAL	N/A	N/A

13. Source of Investment Capital *(personal funds, corporate funds, loans, stocks, debentures, bonds, etc.)*; Evidence of Possession and Control of Funds in the United States *(Attach full documentation)* N/A

PART II - STAFF

14. Type of Personnel in the United States *(Attach staffing chart)*
Specify: [ ] Calendar Year [ ] Fiscal Year

	MANAGERIAL EXECUTIVE		SPECIALIZED ESSENTIAL		ALL OTHER EMPLOYEES	
	This Year	Next Year	This Year	Next Year	This Year	Next Year
Nationals of Treaty Country on E, H, & L Visas:	1	1	1	2	0	0
U.S. Citizens and Legal Permanent Residents:	0	0	0	0	1	1
Other (Third-Country Nationals):	0	0	0	0	0	0
TOTAL:	1	1	1	2	1	1

15. List all personnel of U.S. business holding executive, managerial and/or specialist positions by subsidiary/branch office. If aliens, indicate nonimmigrant visa status or lawful permanent resident (LPR) status.

NAME AND POSITION/TITLE/DIVISION	NATIONALITY	U.S. VISA TYPE	DATE (mm-dd-yyyy)	PLACE OF ISSUANCE
[redacted] President & CEO	Australian	E-1	06-05-2014	USA

PART III - APPLICANT

16. Name of Applicant
(Family Name) ████ (First Name) Peter (Middle Name) ████████

17. Type of Applicant:
☐ Principal owner/investor/trader ☐ Supervisor ☒ Specialist
☐ Manager ☐ Executive ☐ Other

18. Present Position and Duties (Describe in detail).

N/A

19. Name and Address of Employer **N/A**

20. Years with Present Employer	21. Highest Level of Education School	Major/Subject	Degree	Year
N/A	Marymount California University	Business	N/A	2014

22. Other Relevant Experience and Education (Attach Curriculum Vitae - Optional)

See Attached Curriculum Vitae.

23. Position in the United States Title **Department Head of Technology**

Description of duties (include names and titles of all immediate subordinates)

Adapt HMI (Human Machine Interface) and PLC (Programmable Logix Controller) programing software to over 1,000 machines in the Los Angeles area alone.

See attached.

24. Annual U.S. Salary and Benefit Package

39,000 Salary
N/A Allowances/Benefits
39,000 TOTAL

25. Name of Person in the United States Being Replaced N/A

Type of Visa N/A
Date Issued (mm-dd-yyyy)
Place Issued N/A

If NOT a replacement, is this:
a. An increase in staff? ☒ Yes ☐ No
b. Continuation of existing employment in the United States? ☐ Yes ☒ No

26. I do solemnly swear or affirm that all statements which appear in this application are true and complete to the best of my knowledge and belief.

████ Signature of Responsible Officer — ████ President & CEO, Printed Name and Position or Office — 09-01-2015 Date (mm-dd-yyyy)

27. Name and Address of Person Who May be Contacted About This Application

████

VISA FEE RECEIPT

payments made easy

Transaction Number:

Transaction Receipt: Approved

27 August 2015 04:24:13 AEST

Purchase Amount	AUD 266.50
Payment Status	**Approved**
Charged by Merchant	CGI Federal
eWAY Transaction Number	1
Bank Authorisation Code	
Bank Response	**Transaction Approved**

Customer Details

Email	1@live.com

Transaction Details

Invoice Description	US MRV FEE
Invoice Number	
Merchant ID	
Terminal ID	
Card Type	Visa

Transaction processed successfully

Your secure payment was successfully processed by eWAY.

FORM G-28
TAS
AMERICA

Notice of Entry of Appearance as Attorney or Accredited Representative

Department of Homeland Security

DHS Form G-28
OMB No. 1615-0105
Expires 03/31/2018

Part 1. Information About Attorney or Accredited Representative

1. USCIS ELIS Account Number *(if any)* ► [ ]

Name and Address of Attorney or Accredited Representative

2.a. Family Name *(Last Name)* [redacted]

2.b. Given Name *(First Name)* [redacted]

2.c. Middle Name [redacted]

3.a. Street Number and Name: 3233 E Broadway

3.b. Apt. ☐ Ste. ☐ Flr. ☐

3.c. City or Town: Long Beach

3.d. State: CA 3.e. ZIP Code: 90803

3.f. Province

3.g. Postal Code

3.h. Country: USA

4. Daytime Telephone Number [redacted]

5. Fax Number [redacted]

6. E-Mail Address *(if any)* [redacted]

7. Mobile Telephone Number *(if any)*

Part 2. Notice of Appearance as Attorney or Accredited Representative

This appearance relates to immigration matters before *(Select only one box)*:

1.a. ☐ USCIS

1.b. List the form numbers

2.a. ☐ ICE

2.b. List the specific matter in which appearance is entered

3.a. ☐ CBP

3.b. List the specific matter in which appearance is entered

I enter my appearance as attorney or accredited representative at the request of:

4. Select **only one** box:

☐ Applicant ☒ Petitioner ☐ Requestor

☐ Respondent (ICE, CBP)

Information About Applicant, Petitioner, Requestor, or Respondent

5.a. Family Name *(Last Name)*

5.b. Given Name *(First Name)*

5.c. Middle Name

6. Name of Company or Organization *(if applicable)*: [redacted] Inc / TAS America

Part 2. Notice of Appearance as Attorney or Accredited Representative (continued)

Information About Applicant, Petitioner, Requestor, or Respondent (continued)

7. USCIS ELIS Account Number *(if any)*

8. Alien Registration Number (A-Number) or Receipt Number

9. Daytime Telephone Number [redacted]

10. Mobile Telephone Number *(if any)* [redacted]

11. E-Mail Address *(if any)* mel@tasamerica.com

Mailing Address of Applicant, Petitioner, Requestor, or Respondent

NOTE: Provide the mailing address of the applicant, petitioner, requestor, or respondent. If the applicant, petitioner, requestor, or respondent has used a safe mailing address on the application, petition, or request being filed with this Form G-28, provide it in these spaces.

12.a. Street Number and Name [redacted]

12.b. Apt. ☐ Ste. ☐ Flr. ☐

12.c. City or Town [redacted]

12.d. State CA 12.e. ZIP Code [redacted]

12.f. Province

12.g. Postal Code

12.h. Country USA

Part 3. Eligibility Information for Attorney or Accredited Representative

Select **all applicable** items.

1.a. ☒ I am an attorney eligible to practice law in, and a member in good standing of, the bar of the highest courts of the following states, possessions, territories, commonwealths, or the District of Columbia. *(If you need additional space, use **Part 6.**)*

Licensing Authority California Supreme Court

1.b. Bar Number *(if applicable)* [redacted]

1.c. Name of Law Firm [redacted]

1.d. I *(choose one)* ☒ *am not* ☐ *am*

subject to any order of any court or administrative agency disbarring, suspending, enjoining, restraining, or otherwise restricting me in the practice of law. If you are subject to any orders, explain in the space below. *(If you need additional space, use **Part 6.**)*

2.a. ☐ I am an accredited representative of the following qualified nonprofit religious, charitable, social service, or similar organization established in the United States, so recognized by the Department of Justice, Board of Immigration Appeals, in accordance with 8 CFR 292.2. Provide the name of the organization and the expiration date of accreditation.

2.b. Name of Recognized Organization

2.c. Date accreditation expires *(mm/dd/yyyy)* ▶

Part 3. Eligibility Information for Attorney or Accredited Representative *(continued)*

3. ☐ I am associated with

[ ],

the attorney or accredited representative of record who previously filed Form G-28 in this case, and my appearance as an attorney or accredited representative is at his or her request.

NOTE: If you select this item, also complete **Item Numbers 1.a. - 1.b.** or **Item Numbers 2.a. - 2.c.** in **Part 3.** *(whichever is appropriate).*

4.a. ☐ I am a law student or law graduate working under the direct supervision of the attorney or accredited representative of record on this form in accordance with the requirements in 8 CFR 292.1(a)(2)(iv).

4.b. Name of Law Student or Law Graduate

[ ]

Part 4. Applicant, Petitioner, Requestor, or Respondent Consent to Representation, Contact Information, and Signature

Consent to Representation and Release of Information

1. I have requested the representation of and consented to being represented by the attorney or accredited representative named in **Part 1.** of this form. According to the Privacy Act of 1974 and DHS policy, I also consent to the disclosure to the named attorney or accredited representative of any record pertaining to me that appears in any system of records of USCIS, ICE or CBP.

When you (the applicant, petitioner, requestor, or respondent) are represented, DHS will send notices to both you and your attorney or accredited representative either through mail or electronic delivery.

DHS will also send the Form I-94, Arrival Departure Record, to you unless you select **Item Number 2.a.** in **Part 4.** All secure identity documents and Travel Documents will be sent to you (the applicant, petitioner, requestor, or respondent) unless you ask us to send those documents to your attorney of record or accredited representative.

If you do not want to receive original notices or secure identity documents directly, but would rather have such notices and documents sent to your attorney of record or accredited representative, please select **all applicable** boxes below:

2.a ☐ I request DHS send any notice (including Form I-94) on an application, petition, or request to the business address of my attorney of record or accredited re[redacted]sentative as listed in this form. I understand that I [redacted] change this election at any future date through w[redacted]en notice to DHS.

2.b. ☐ I request that DHS send any secure identity document, such as a Permanent Resident Card, Employment Authorization Document, or Travel Document, that I am approved to receive and authorized to possess, to the business address of my attorney of record or accredited representative as listed in this form. I consent to having my secure identity document sent to my attorney of record accredited representative and understand that I [redacted] request, at any future date and through written [redacted]ce to DHS, that DHS send any secure identity document to me directly.

3.a. Signature of Applicant, Petitioner, Requestor, or Respondent

3.b. Date of Signature *(mm/dd/yyyy)* ► 09/01/2015

Part 5. Signature of Attorney or Accredited Representative

I have read and understand the regulations and conditions contained in 8 CFR 103.2 and 292 governing appearances and representation before the Department of Homeland Security. I declare under penalty of perjury under the laws of the United States that the information I have provided on this form is true and correct.

1. Signature of Attorney or Accredited Representative

2. Signature of Law Student or Law Graduate

[ ]

3. Date of Signature *(mm/dd/yyyy)* ► 09/01/2015

Part 6. Additional Information

Use the space below to provide additional information pertaining to **Part 3., Item Numbers 1.a. - 1.d.**

Form G-28 03/04/15 N

FORM G-28

Notice of Entry of Appearance as Attorney In Matters Outside the Geographical Confines of the United States

Department of Homeland Security

DHS Form G-28I
OMB No. 1615-0105
Expires 03/31/2018

Part 1. Information About Attorney

1. USCIS ELIS Account Number *(if any)*

Name and Address of Attorney

2.a. Family Name *(Last Name)*
2.b. Given Name *(First Name)*
2.c. Middle Name
3. Name of Law Firm *(if applicable)*
4.a. Street Number and Name
4.b. Apt. ☐ Ste. ☐ Flr. ☐
4.c. City or Town
4.d. Province
4.e. Postal Code
4.f. Country
USA
5. Telephone Number
6. Fax Number
7. E-Mail Address *(if any)*
8. Mobile Telephone Number *(if any)*

Part 2. Notice of Appearance as Attorney Admitted to Practice Outside the United States

This appearance relates to immigration matters before *(select **only one** box)*:

1.a. ☐ USCIS
1.b. List the form numbers
2.a. ☐ ICE
2.b. List the specific matter in which appearance is entered
3.a. ☐ CBP
3.b. List the specific matter in which appearance is entered

I enter my appearance as attorney at the request of:

4. Select **only one** box:
☒ Applicant ☐ Petitioner ☐ Respondent (ICE, CBP)

Information About Applicant, Petitioner, or Respondent

5.a. Family Name *(Last Name)*
5.b. Given Name
5.c. Middle Name
6. Name of Company or Organization *(if applicable)*
7. USCIS ELIS Account Number *(if any)*
8. Alien Registration Number (A-Number) or Receipt Number (if any)
9. Telephone Number
10. E-Mail Address *(if any)*
live.com

Part 2. Notice of Appearance as Attorney Admitted to Practice Outside the United States (continued)

Mailing Address

NOTE: Provide the mailing address of the applicant, petitioner, or respondent. If the applicant, petitioner, or respondent has used a safe mailing address on the application or petition being filed with this Form G-28I, provide it in these spaces.

11.a. Street Number and Name [redacted]

11.b. Apt. ☐ Ste. ☐ Flr. ☐

11.c. City or Town [redacted]

11.d. Province [redacted]

11.e. Postal Code [redacted]

11.f. Country

Australia

Part 3. Eligibility Information for Attorney

Select **all applicable** boxes.

1.a. ☒ I am licensed and authorized to practice law in the following countries. *(If you need additional space, use Part 6.)*

Licensing Authority

California Supreme Court

1.b. Bar Number *(if applicable)*

1.c. ☐ I am in good standing in a court of general jurisdiction in the following countries where I reside and am engaged in the practice of law. *(If you need additional space, use Part 6.)*

1.d. I *(choose one)* ☐ *am not* ☐ *am* subject to any order of any court or administrative agency disbarring, suspending, enjoining, restraining, or otherwise restricting me in the practice of law. If you are subject to any orders, explain in the space below. *(If you need additional space, use Part 6.)*

2. ☐ I am associated with

the attorney of record who previously filed Form G-28I in this case, and my appearance as an attorney is at his or her request.

NOTE: If you select this item, also complete **Item Numbers 1.a. - 1.c.**

Part 4. Applicant, Petitioner, or Respondent Consent to Representation, Contact Information, and Signature

Consent to Representation and Release of Information

1. I have requested the representation of and consented to being represented by the attorney named in **Part 1.** of this form. According to the Privacy Act of 1974 and DHS policy, I also consent to the disclosure to the named attorney of any record pertaining to me that appears in any system of records of USCIS, ICE, or CBP.

When you (the applicant, petitioner, requestor, or respondent) are represented, DHS will send notices to both you and your attorney either through mail or electronic delivery.

DHS will also send the Form I-94, Arrival Departure Record, to you **unless** you select **Item Number 2.a. in Part 4.** All secure identity documents and Travel Documents will be sent to you (the applicant, petitioner, requestor, or respondent) unless you ask us to send those documents to your attorney of record.

If you do not want to receive original notices or secure identity documents directly, but would rather have such notices and documents sent to your attorney of record, please select **all applicable** boxes below:

2.a. ☐ I request that DHS send any notice (including Form I-94) on an application, petition, or request that I have filed with DHS to the business address of my attorn[redacted]f record as listed in this form. I understand that I [redacted] change this election at any future date throug[redacted] ritten notice to DHS.

Part 4. Applicant, Petitioner, or Respondent Consent to Representation, Contact Information, and Signature *(continued)*

2.b. ☐ I request that DHS send any secure identity document, such as a Permanent Resident Card, Employment Authorization Document, or Travel Document, that I am approved to receive and authorized to possess, to the business address of my attorney of record as listed in this form. I consent to having my secure identity document sent to my attorney of record and understand that I [redacted] request, at any future date and through written notice to DHS, that DHS send any secure identity document to me directly.

3.a. Signature of Applicant, Petitioner, or Respondent

3.b. Date of Signature *(mm/dd/yyyy)* ► 09/01/2015

Part 5. Signature of Attorney

I have read and understand the regulations and conditions contained in 8 CFR 103.2 and 292 governing appearances and representation before the Department of Homeland Security. I declare under penalty of perjury under the laws of the United States that the information I have provided on this form is true and correct.

1.a. Signatur ey

1.b. Date of Signature *(mm/dd/yyyy)* ► 09/01/2015

Part 6. Additional Information

Use the space provided below to provide additional information pertaining to **Part 3., Item Numbers 1.a. - 1.c.**

JOB LETTER

TAS AMERICA 1425 1ST STREET SAN FERNANDO CA 91340

To Whom It [redacted] Concern, AUGUST 1ST 2015

[redacted] Inc. doing business as TAS America was established in 2009 in California by [redacted] [redacted] for the purpose of importing screen printing machinery and parts from TAS International, a registered company in Australia, and selling and servicing TAS International screen printing machines and products in the United States. However, in recent years, difficulties in finding qualified U.S. employees have prevented us from maintaining our desired level of service and back-up support to our client base. This and other factors have led to a reduction in the volume of our business. Thus, to improve on this situation and boost our company expertise we wish to hire an individual who has trained to become an expert in TAS products.

Our aim is to restore our former volume of business and maintain our valued name in the U.S. market while at the same time satisfying our customers through continued improvement of all aspects of our business. To achieve this, we propose to appoint Mr. [redacted] as Department Head of Technology of TAS America with an annual salary of $39,000 per year. Mr. [redacted] is an excellent candidate for this position as he has a strong understanding of the HMI (Human Machine Interface) and PLC (Programmable Logic Controller) programing software and will help adapt this technology to over 1,000 machines in the Los Angeles area alone.

Mr. [redacted] Experience:

Four Years of Training on TAS Equipment

Extensive Experience and Knowledge with Assembly/Disassembly of TAS Equipment

Certification in IDEC Basic and Advanced Programming

Familiarity with Southern California

Knowledge and Close Relationships with American Customers

Three Years of Education in Management and Small Business

Developed and Awarded for New Ideas on TAS Equipment

Sales Experience with TAS Machinery

Given these skills, knowledge and experience, which cannot be found in the U.S. workforce, Mr. ███ is an ideal candidate to work for TAS America. As Department Head of Technology, Mr. ███ will not only assist in the adaption of new technology in our machines dating from 1982-1999 but will also be responsible for the following:

Adapting IDEC technology to later model machinery consisting of over 1,000 machines in the Los Angeles area

Overseeing new designs or ideas

Sourcing products needed from American manufacturing companies

Handling day-to-day instruction specifically to HMI and PLC installation and repair

Dealing with customer service issues

Acting as a contact between TAS International and TAS America

Mr. ███ knowledge and experience is hard to come by in someone so young and passionate. His experience will be useful in the advancement and growth of the TAS America. Mr. ███ has applied for an appropriate working visa to allow himself to take up this offer and we would be grateful if you could give this application your favorable support as our company will only benefit with Mr. ███ as an employee.

We trust that we have furnished all of the information needed by you to process this application but should you require any further assistance please do not hesitate to contact us.

Thank you for your assistance in this matter.

Respectfully,

EXHIBITS

PASSPORT (BIO Data Page), I-94s and VISA

Form I-797A (Rev. 10/31/05) N
OBSERVATIONS
PASSPORT
AUSTRALIA
DOCUMENT No.
P
AUS
AUSTRALIAN
08 APR 1993
M
02 FEB 2022
AUSTRALIA
P<<<<<<<<
N
0

DISTRITO FEDERAL
MEXICO 2010

CHIP CENTRE PAGE
This passport contains sensitive electronics. For best performance, please do not bend, perforate or expose to extreme temperatures or excess moisture.
DO NOT STAMP THIS PAGE
This passport contains a contactless integrated circuit chip which is an electronic device. In addition to the normal care and respect afforded a passport, please regard this document as you would any other portable electronic device, by ensuring that it does not become wet, folded or mutilated. Abuse
adversely affect the operation of the chip and reduce its utility to the bearer and to border inspection personnel.
Form I-797A (Rev. 10/31/05) N

U.S. Customs and Border Protection
Securing America's Borders

OMB No. 1651-0111
Expiration Date: 06/30/2015

Most Recent I-94

Admission (I-94) Record Number: [redacted]

Most Recent Date of Entry: 2015 [redacted] **16**

Class of Admission: WT

Admit Until Date: 08/13/2015

Details provided on the I-94 Information form:

Last/Surname:	[redacted]
First (Given) Name:	[redacted] W
Birth Date:	**1993 April 08**
Passport Number:	[redacted]
Country of Issuance:	**Australia**

[Get Travel History]

▶ Effective April 26, 2013, DHS began automating the admission process. An alien lawfully admitted or paroled into the U.S. is no longer required to be in possession of a preprinted Form I-94. A record of admission printed from the CBP website constitutes a lawful record of admission. See 8 CFR § 1.4(d).

▶ If an employer, local, state or federal agency requests admission information, present your admission (I-94) number along with any additional required documents requested by that employer or agency

▶ Note: For security reasons, we recommend that you close your browser after you have finished retrieving your I-94 number.

For inquiries or questions regarding your I-94, please click here.

Accessibility | Privacy Policy

Detach This Half for Personal Records

Receip [illegible]
I-94#
NAME
CLASS

VALID FROM 07/21/2014 UNTIL DS
Valid for Duration of Status
PETITIONER: MAY, PETER J.
818 [illegible]LEN AVENUE
GLENDALE CA 91201

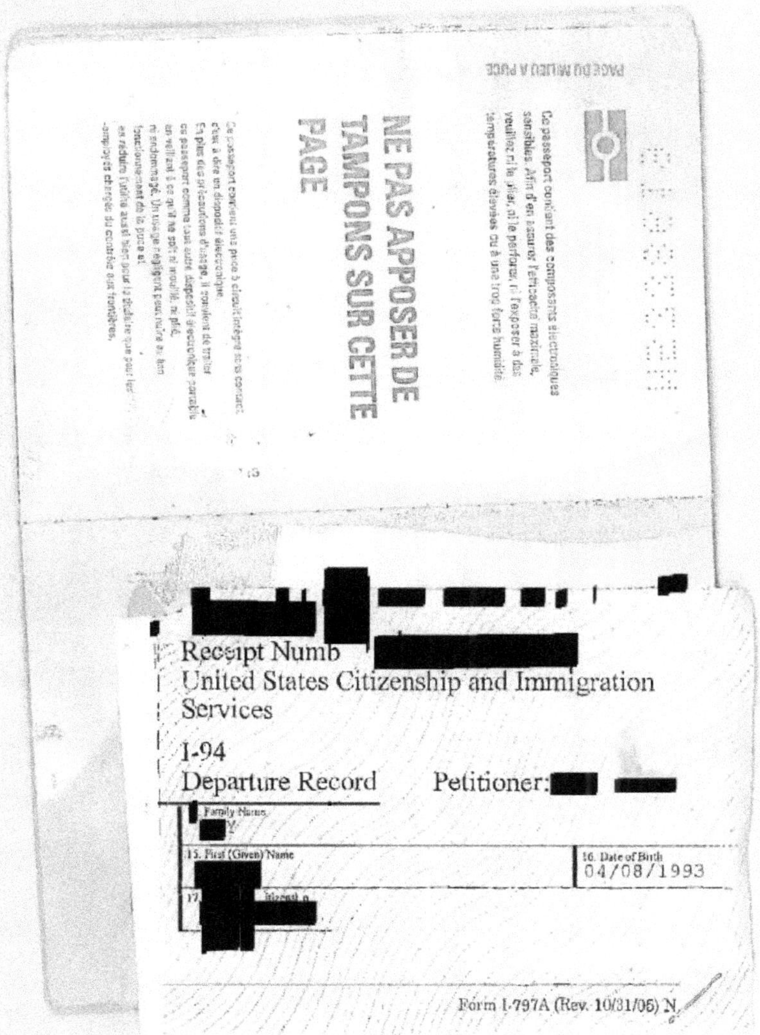
NE PAS APPOSER DE TAMPONS SUR CETTE PAGE

Receipt Numb

United States Citizenship and Immigration Services

I-94

Departure Record Petitioner:

Family Name

15. First (Given) Name

16. Date of Birth

04/08/1993

Form I-797A (Rev. 10/31/05) N

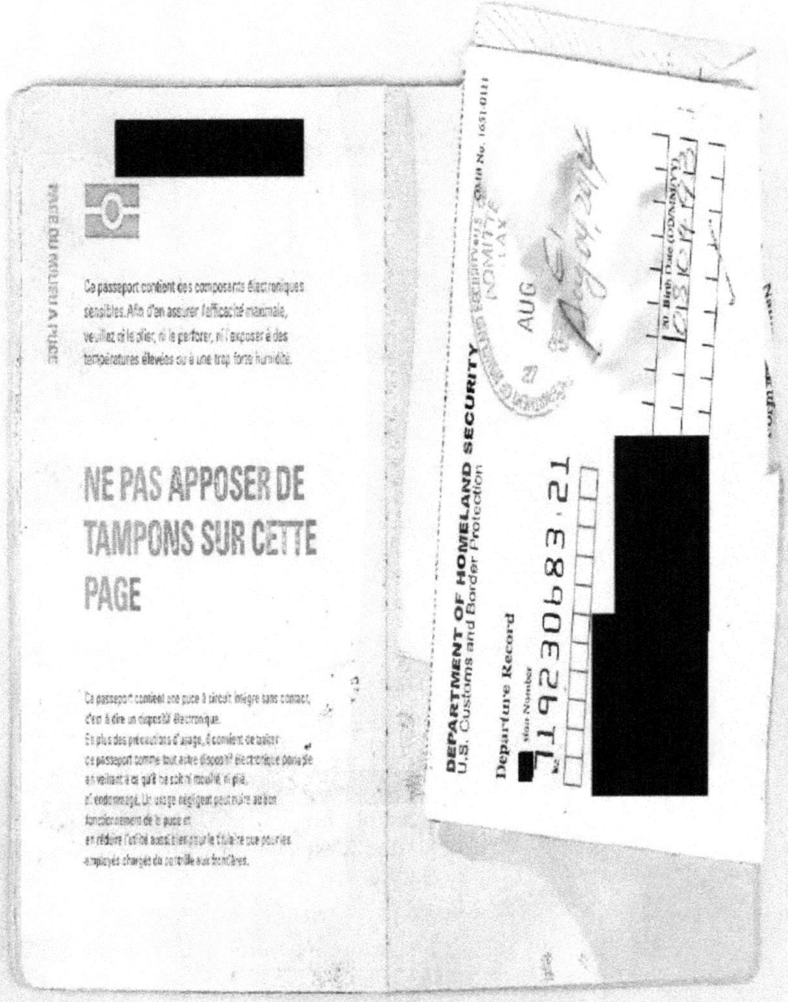
NE PAS APPOSER DE
TAMPONS SUR CETTE
PAGE
DEPARTMENT OF HOMELAND SECURITY
U.S. Customs and Border Protection
Departure Record

VISA
UNITED STATES OF AMERICA
NAY
Visa Type/Class
R E1
Birth Date
Nationality
M6273593
M
Entries
M
1000
PA:
J
SEP 2 6 2010
E-1
28 Sep 2012
JAN 0 9 2009
E1
Jan 08 2011

RESUME OR CURRICULUM VITAE

live.com

"Failure is simply the opportunity to begin again, this time more intelligently."
Henry Ford

My Objective:

I believe that through hard work and intelligent ideas, success will come. My objective is to utilize my college education and what I have learned over the past seven years, helping my parents with their company TAS America, to a management position in the same industry I grew up in. I wish to relate my mother and father's work to my own so that I myself reach a higher level of expertise. The skills and experience that I have gained learning with TAS machinery is extremely useful in the business world. With TAS machines no two problems are the same, a lot like business. This is why each problem I run into will require individual attention. No problem is too small when it comes to customers and every customers deserves an answer.

My Experience:

I have gained many years of experience on working with machinery and components of the Silk Screen Industry. I have been around a successful small business all my life. From birth util I was fourteen year old, my parents owned a silk screen company that printed shirts for companies like Nike, Adidas, and many more. From the age of fourteen until now, my parents have owned TAS america a company that specializes in selling silkscreen machinery to other businesses, a lot like the business they used to own. My life has been all about business and what goes on inside a business. I have experience with customers at various expos, where I have explained and shown how silkscreen equipment works and how it can be used in other industries other than t-shirt and direct to garment.

I have also volunteered for a nursery in San Pedro, CA where I learned about patience and taking instructions about something new and unfamiliar. The skills I learned from this experience will help me give better instruction to people underneath me and providing patience with anyone whom might learn from me, while also being patient to learn something from someone else.

My Education:

Three years of business school, attending Marymount California University and Moorpark Community College.

(Focus)

-Entrepreneurship
-Management
-Economics
-Business Plan Preparation
-Business Law
-Small Business Start-up

(Special Projects in College)

Garbology Project - Investigated the garbage problem in Los Angeles and other parts of America. Visiting waste management facilities in Torrance and Santa Ana we were able to come up with solutions to solve the problem. Each member of the team sent a letter to the San Pedro government including our ideas and solutions, a lot of us including myself were sent a letter in return thanking us for our input.

Small Business Project - Three other students and myself were given a project to create a business that could be successful in this economy and plan out every detail of the business until actually paying for rent and getting a business license. We had to pitch the business to a group of teachers from the business program at Marymount California University. My group was awarded second place.

(Memberships in College)

-MCU Golf Team
-Moorpark International Student Group

(Volunteering)

-Boys and Girls club in San Pedro, California
-San Pedro Nursery

(Certificate of Completion)

-IDEC PLC-HMI Basic and Advanced Programming
-QPR Suicide Prevention Training
-Certified in CPR and Emergency Care

<u>My Skills:</u>

-Welding
-Carpentry Experience
-Quickbooks
-PhotoShop
-Excel
-IDEC Programming Software
-Forklift Driver
-TAS Machine Assembly and Repair
-Excavator Experience
-TAS Machine Crate Assembly and Manufacturing

LETTER OF INTENT TO DEPART

September 3, 2015

U.S. Consulate General Melbourne
553 St. Kilda Road
Melbourne, VIC 3004

Re: E-1 Treaty Trador (Employee/Essential Skills)
Petitioner: [redacted] Inc. dba TAS America
Beneficiary/Applicant: [redacted]

To Whom it [redacted] Concern:

This letter is to confirm that it is my full intention to depart the United States and return to Australia upon expiration of any E-1 visa/status granted to me.

Sincerely,

SECTION 4: Ownership of Business

This section should display proof of the ownership you possess over your business.

This should include:

* Articles of Incorporation
* Fictitious Name Statement
* Share Certificate

ARTICLES OF INCORPORATION

3188496

State of California
Secretary of State

I, DEBRA BOWEN, Secretary of State of the State of California, hereby certify:

That the attached transcript of 1 page(s) has been compared with the record on file in this office, of which it purports to be a copy, and that it is full, true and correct.

IN WITNESS WHEREOF, I execute this certificate and affix the Great Seal of the State of California this day of

FEB 1 9 2009

3188496

ENDORSED - FILED
In the office of the Secretary of State
of the State of California

FEB 13 2009

ARTICLES OF INCORPORATION

ARTICLE I

The name of this corporation is [redacted] Inc.

ARTICLE II

The purpose of this corporation is to engage in any lawful act or activity for which a corporation [redacted] be organized under the General Corporation Law of California other than the banking business, the trust company business or the practice of a profession permitted to be incorporated by the California Corporations Code.

ARTICLE III

The name and address in the State of California of this corporation's initial agent for service of process is:

ARTICLE IV

This corporation is authorized to issue only one class of shares of stock; and the total number of shares which the corporation is authorized to issue is one million (1,000,000).

ARTICLE V

The liability of directors of the corporation for monetary damages shall be eliminated to the fullest extent permissible under California law. The corporation is authorized to provide indemnification of agents (as defined in Section 317 of the California Corporations Code) through Bylaw provisions, agreements with agents, vote of shareholders or disinterested directors, or otherwise, to the fullest extent permissible under California law. Any amendment, repeal or modification of this provision of this Article V shall not adversely affect any right or protection of an agent of this corporation existing at the time of such amendment, repeal or modification.

Dated: February 12, 2009

[redacted] Incorporator

OFFICE OF THE

FICTITIOUS NAME STATEMENT

Recorded Mail Document To:

TAS AMERICA
30304 Mallorca Place
Castaic, CA 91384

This space is for the County Clerk's Filing Stamp

04/22/2009

20090587996

PROOF OF PUBLICATION

PROOF OF PUBLICATION
(2015.5 C.C.P)

STATE OF CALIFORNIA,
COUNTY OF LOS ANGELES,

I am a citizen of the United States and a resident of the County aforesaid; I am over the age of eighteen years, and not a party to or interested in the above-entitled matter. I am the principal clerk of the printer of the

THE TOLUCAN TIMES AND CANYON CRIER

a newspaper of general circulation, printed and published **WEEKLY**

in the City of **TOLUCA LAKE**

County of Los Angeles, and which newspaper has been adjudged a newspaper of general circulation by the superior Court of the County of Los Angeles, State of California, under the date of

29, 1956

Case Number N that the notice of which the annexed is a printed copy (set in type not smaller than nonpareil), has been published in each regular and entire issue of said newspaper and not in any supplement thereof on the following dates, to wit"

03-27-09, 04-03-09, 04-10-09, 04-17-09

Dated at **TOLUCA LAKE**
California, on April 17, 2009

SIGNATURE

Proof of Publication of File # **2009-0297071**

FICTITIOUS BUSINESS NAME(S):

TAS AMERICA

FICTITIOUS NAME STATEMENT 2009-0297071

The following person(s) are doing business as: **TAS AMERICA , 30304 Mallorca Place, Castaic, CA 91384.** The full name of registrant(s) is/are: **Inc, 30304 Mallorca Place, Castaic, CA 91384.** This business is conducted by a **corporation**. I declare that all information in this statement is true and correct. (A registrant who declares as true information which he or she knows to be false is guilty of a crime.) Signed: **President**. Have you started doing business?: **N/A.** This statement was filed with the County Clerk of Los Angeles County on (Date) **March 3, 2009.** NOTICE: This fictitious name statement expires five years from the date it was filed in the office of the county clerk. A new fictitious business name statement must be filed before that time. The filing of this statement does not of itself authorize the use in this state of a fictitious business name in violation of the rights of another under federal, state, or common

THE TOLUCAN TIMES AND CANYON CRIER CERTIFIES THAT THE ABOVE FICTITIOUS NAME HAS BEEN PUBLISHED FOUR TIMES ON THE ABOVE-MENTIONED DATES

This page is part of your do[illegible]nt - DO NOT DISCARD

Pages: 0002

Recorded/Filed in Official Records
Recorder's Office, Los Angeles County,
California

04/22/09 AT 01:54PM

FEES:	0.00
TAXES:	0.00
OTHER:	0.00
PAID:	0.00

LEADSHEET

200904220480011

00000403984

002073695

SEQ:
13

DAR - Counter (Hard Copy)

SHARE CERTIFICATE

FEBRUARY 13, 2009

INCORPORATED UNDER THE LAWS OF THE STATE OF CALIFORNIA

NUMBER	SHARES
1	--100,000--

May National, Inc.

AUTHORIZED: 1,000,000 SHARES COMMON STOCK

This Certifies that [redacted] is the registered holder of ---One Hundred Thousand----- Shares of the above named Corporation transferable only on the books of the Corporation by the holder hereof in person or by Attorney upon surrender of this Certificate properly endorsed.

In Witness Whereof, the said Corporation has caused this Certificate to be signed by its duly authorized officers and its Corporate Seal to be hereunto affixed this 16th day of February A.D. 2009

[redacted] SECRETARY

[redacted] PRESIDENT

"THE SHARES REPRESENTED BY THIS CERTIFICATE HAVE NOT BEEN REGISTERED UNDER THE SECURITIES ACT OF 1933, AS AMENDED, AND HAVE BEEN ACQUIRED FOR INVESTMENT AND NOT WITH A VIEW TO THE SALE OR DISTRIBUTION THEREOF. NO SUCH SALE OR DISTRIBUTION ████ BE EFFECTED WITHOUT AN EFFECTIVE REGISTRATION STATEMENT RELATING THERETO OR AN OPINION OF COUNSEL OR OTHER EVIDENCE SATISFACTORY TO THE ISSUER THAT SUCH REGISTRATION IS NOT REQUIRED."

For Value Received, ______ *hereby sell, assign and transfer unto* ____

____ *Shares represented by the within Certificate, and do hereby irrevocably constitute and appoint*

____ *Attorney to transfer the said Shares on the books of the within named Corporation with full power of substitution in the premises.*

Dated ____________________

In presence of

__________________________ __________________________

NOTICE: THE SIGNATURE OF THIS ASSIGNMENT MUST CORRESPOND WITH THE NAME AS WRITTEN UPON THE FACE OF THE CERTIFICATE, IN EVERY PARTICULAR, WITHOUT ALTERATION OR ENLARGEMENT OR ANY CHANGE WHATEVER.

Trade

You must be able to show that your company has been involved in trade. This section should depict any spreadsheets depicting where your company was involved in trade. This can be international spreadsheets, airbills or shipping invoices. You shall see examples of these in use.

2014
INTERNATIONAL TRADE SPREADSHEET

2014 INTERNATIONL TRADE

DATE	INVOICE	DOLLAR AMOUNT
01/31/14	2224	$54,000.00
04/15/14	12729	$1,378.00
06/06/14	12764	$2,076.20
06/11/14	12769	$678.60
06/26/14	12788	$386.50
07/10/14	12803	$446.38
08/15/14	12833	$915.76
09/30/14	12867	$2,007.65
10/10/14	12881	$50,250.00
10/10/14	12882	$43,262.00
10/14/14	12833	$48,250.00
10/17/14	12877	$450.00
10/17/14	12877	$2,127.84
10/29/14	12902	$122,250.00
11/17/14	12909	$233.24
11/21/14	12912	$353.24
12/02/14	12645	$375.00
12/11/14	12933	$252.00
12/11/14	12934	$2,277.71
12/18/14	12946	$61,000.00
12/19/14	2247/2248/2250	$141,762.00
TOTAL		**TOTAL**
21		$534,732.12

2014 INVOICES

TAS INTERNATIONAL
TAS SCREEN PRINTING EQUIPMENT PTY LTD – A.B.N. 85 006 692 351

www.tasinternational.com.au

COMMERCIAL INVOICE

INVOICE NO.:	2224
DATE:	31/01/2014
CUST. REF / PO #:	246

INVOICE TO:
TAS AMERICA

U.S.A
TEL:

SHIP TO:
TAS AMERICA

U.S.A

DESCRIPTION OF GOODS AND/OR SERVICES	UNIT PRICE	QUANTITY	TOTAL
1 X NEW 'TAS' AUTOMATIC SCREEN PRINTING MACHINE & ACCESSORIES;	$54,000.00	1	USD 54,000.00
MODEL : COMPACT CX12			
SERIAL NO. : 1295			
INCLUDES STANDARD ACCESSORIES:			
SET OF (14) ADULT QUICK RELEASE ALUMINIUM PALLETS - 470MM X 610MM		14	
SET OF (12) SQUEEGEES W/RUBBER RED STANDARD - 460MM		12	
SET OF (12) FIG7 FLOODBARS STANDARD - 460MM		12	
PRINT AREA - 457MM X 508MM & MAX SCREEN SIZE - 610MM X 762MM			
AC ELECTRIC ROTATION AND PRINT HEADS			
CENTRAL OFF CONTACT & ROTO PRINT PROGRAM			
INDIVIDUAL HEAD OFF CONTACT & PNEUMATIC CLAMPING			
MULTI- FUNCTIONAL FOOT SWITCH & SKIP SHIRT AND PAUSE PEDAL			
FRONT, CENTRE AND REAR MICRO REGISTRATION			
MACHINE ELECTRICAL REQUIREMENTS - 220V/ 3PHASE			
PACKING & CRATING			
SHIPPING TO CIF LONG BEACH PORT, U.S.A			
FREIGHT TERMS : PREPAID - CIF LONG BEACH PORT			
PAYMENT TERMS : 50% DEPOSIT ON ORDER & BALANCE TO BE PAID PRIOR TO SHIPMENT			
MANUFACTURED IN VICTORIA, AUSTRALIA ***COUNTRY OF ORIGIN AUSTRALIA***	SUBTOTAL		USD 54,000.00
	TOTAL, CIF LONG BEACH		**USD 54,000.00**

Warranty Terms: Full warranty period (2-yr) covers parts manufactured solely by TAS.. Commercially bought in parts (Motors, Gear Boxes, Inverters etc) are covered by the manufacturers standard 12 month warranty period only.

Beneficiary's Telegraphic Transfer Bank Account Details:
(Please note that all bank charges or fees outside of Australia are to be borne by customer)

Account Name:	395814USD00001
Account number:	013024
BSB Number:	ANZBAU3M
SWIFT Code:	ANZ BANK

TAS International
TAS SCREEN PRINTING EQUIPMENT PTY LTD

Phone: 61 3 9587 2600
Fax: 61 3 9587 2789
ABN: 85 006 692 351

Tax Invoice No. 12729

Page 1 of 1

Invoice Address: TAS AMERICA
1425 First Street,
San Fernando, CA 91340
U.S.A.
Phone:
Fax:

Shipping Address: TAS AMERICA
1425 First Street,
San Fernando, CA 91340
U.S.A.
Phone:

Ship Via	Tracking Number	Despatch Date	Shipment No	Picking/Pro Inv. No
Federal Express	5622 3531 3879	15/04/2014	12230	12707

Invoice Date	Due Date	Payment Terms	Your Order	Salesperson
15/04/2014	15/04/2014	Cash Before Despatch	290	Hiros C Azid

Part ID / Description:	Order Qty:	U/M:	Unit Price:	Unit Discount:	Extended Price:
200RA-07-01-0AM Pressure Setting Knob-Squ/Fld	100.00	EA	1.50	0.45	USD$105.00
200RA-06-52 Mushroom Buffer (Large) 90 Duro	1,000.00	EA	1.25	0.38	USD$875.00
200RA-12-07-0AM Screen Clamping Foot	200.00	EA	1.95	0.58	USD$273.00

COUNTRY OF ORIGIN - AUSTRALIA

PAYMENT BY T/T - Account Details are:
Account Name: TAS SCREEN PRINTING EQUIPMENT PTY LTD
Account Number:
Swift Code: ANZBAU3M
BSB Number: 013024
Bank Name: ANZ BANK
Branch Address:

Invoice Sub-total	USD$1,253.00
Freight	USD$125.00
INVOICE TOTAL	**USD$1,378.00**

TAS International

Phone:

TAS

Tax Invoice No. 12764

Page 1 of 1

TAS AMERICA
U.S.A.
Phone:
Fax:

Shipping Address: TAS AMERICA

Ship Via	Tracking Number	Despatch Date	Shipment No	Picking/Pro Inv. No
Hand Carry	HAND CARRY BY OTTO	6/06/2014	12257	12726

Invoice Date	Due Date	Payment Terms	Your Order	Salesperson
6/06/2014	6/07/2014	30 Days W/Discount	300	Hiros C Azid

Part ID / Description:	Order Qty:	U/M:	Unit Price:	Unit Discount:	Extended Price:
200RA-12-25-0CM Hand Locknut M12 - Plastic	50.00	EA	3.95	1.18	USD$138.25
200RA-08-01-0B Micro-Reg Bush - Plain	40.00	EA	2.86	0.86	USD$80.08
200RA-08-02-0BM Micro Reg Bush Spigotted	80.00	EA	2.86	0.86	USD$160.16
205RA-02-17 Indexer Slotted Plate	1.00	EA	350.00	105.00	USD$245.00
200RA-05-15-0BM Locator Pin	50.00	EA	3.43	1.03	USD$120.05
200RA-06-22 Stroke Limit Clamp	20.00	EA	48.00	14.40	USD$672.00
200RA-06-51 Spacer Collar - Carrier	5.00	EA	15.00	4.50	USD$52.50
200RA-12-20 Clamp Plate	30.00	EA	3.50	1.05	USD$73.50
200RA-07-09 Clamp Angle-Squeegee	50.00	EA	7.62	2.29	USD$266.70
2000-06-16 Printhead Mtg.Clampnut	10.00	EA	14.28	4.28	USD$99.96
OFFCO-14 Jacking Pin	6.00	EA	40.00	12.00	USD$168.00

INVOICE TO BE OFFSET

*****COUNTRY OF ORIGIN - AUSTRALIA*****

PAYMENT BY T/T - Account Details are:

Account Name: TAS SCREEN PRINTING EQUIPMENT PTY LTD
Account Number: 3
Swift Code:
BSB Number: 013024
Bank Name: ANZ BANK
Branch Address: 100 Queen St. Melbourne, VIC, 3000, Australia

BY CREDIT CARD - VISA or MASTER - Please send us your card details

Invoice Sub-total	USD$2,076.20
Freight	USD$0.00
INVOICE TOTAL	**USD$2,076.20**

TAS International

TAS SCREEN PRINTING EQUIPMENT PTY LTD

Phone:

Fax:

ABN:

Tax Invoice No. 12769

Page 1 of 1

Invoice Address: TAS AMERICA

U.S.A.

Phone:

Fax:

Shipping Address: TAS AMERICA

U.S.A.

Phone:

Ship Via	Tracking Number	Despatch Date	Shipment No	Picking/Pro Inv. No
DHL Express	4595321500	11/06/2014	12262	12753

Invoice Date	Due Date	Payment Terms	Your Order	Salesperson
11/06/2014	11/07/2014	30 Days W/Discount	Mel	Hiros C Azid

Part ID / Description	Order Qty:	U/M:	Unit Price:	Unit Discount:	Extended Price:
894254 Piggy Back Cylinder	2.00	EA	360.00	108.00	USD$504.00
SALES P101 Green Seal	40.00	EA	4.45	1.34	USD$124.60

COUNTRY OF ORIGIN - AUSTRALIA

USD$628.60

USD$50.00

USD$678.60

TAS International

Phone:

TAS

Tax Invoice No. 12788

Page 1 of 1

TAS AMERICA
1425 First Street,

Shipping Address: TAS AMERICA

	Tracking Number	Despatch Date	Shipment No	Picking/Pro Inv. No
DHL Express	606684354	26/06/2014	12279	12772

Invoice Date	Due Date	Payment Terms	Your Order	Salesperson
26/06/2014	26/07/2014	30 Days W/Discount	Swap Ccfh13/4Sb	

Part ID / Description:	Order Qty:	U/M:	Unit Price:	Unit Discount:	Extended Price:
200RA-07-02 Squeegee Flood Cylinder 25 x 25mm (Special price as per agreed with Otto)	20.00	EA	55.00	0.00	USD$1,100.00
SALES Offset against TAS America Inv # 6264 (Swap CCFH13/4SB - Cam Follower 1 3/4")	1.00	EA	-840.00	0.00	-USD$840.00
0184 Freight Charges	1.00	EA	115.00	0.00	USD$115.00

COUNTRY OF ORIGIN - AUSTRALIA

Invoice Sub-total	USD$375.00
Freight	USD$0.00
INVOICE TOTAL	**USD$386.50**

2014 AIR BILLS OR SHIPPING INVOICES

Consignor	BILL OF LADING
TAS SCREEN PRINTING EQUIPMENT PTY LTD AUSTRALIA	NOT NEGOTIABLE UNLESS CONSIGNED "TO ORDER"
Consigned to order of TAS AMERICA	Freightnet International INTERNATIONAL FREIGHT FORWARDERS
Notify Address SAME AS CONSIGNEE	Freightnet International (Vic) Pty Ltd

	Place of Receipt MELBOURNE, AUSTRALIA	
Ocean Vessel PESCARA / 367N	Port of loading MELBOURNE, AUSTRALIA	
Port of discharge LOS ANGELES, UNITED STATES	Place of Delivery LOS ANGELES, UNITED STATES	**EXPRESS** Express Bill of Lading

Marks and Numbers	Number and Kind of Packages	Description of Goods	Gross Weight	Measurement
N/A	1	x 20GP CONTAINER 3 Crate(s) 1 x NEW 'TAS' AUTOMATIC SCREEN PRINTING MACHINE & ACCESSORIES MODEL: COMPACT CX12 SERIAL NO: 1295 TERMS: CIF LONG BEACH	2811 KG	15.89 M3

Container	Seals	Type	Weight	Volume	Packages	Mode
DVRU1557652	372411	20GP	2811 KG	15.89 M3	3 CRT	CY/CY*

CAN: ACF6PLATE   Consol Ref: C00034537

Total Packages: ONE CONTAINER(S)   *Shipper Load Count and Sealed

SHIPPED ON BOARD 02-Feb-14   according to the declaration of the consignor

Declaration of Interest of the consignor in timely delivery (Clause 6.2.)	Declared value for ad valorem rate according to the declaration of the consignor (Clauses 7 and 8)

The goods and instructions are accepted and dealt with subject to the Standard Conditions printed overleaf.

Taken in charge in apparent good order and condition, unless otherwise noted herein, at the place of receipt for transport and delivery as mentioned above.

One of these Multimodal Transport Bills of Lading must be surrendered duly endorsed in exchange for the goods. In Witness whereof the original Multimodal Transport Bills of Lading and all of this tenor and date have been signed in the number stated below, one of which being accomplished the other(s) to be void.

Freight amount	Freight Payable at	Place and date of issue
FREIGHT PREPAID	MELBOURNE, AUSTRALIA	MELBOURNE, AUSTRALIA 02-Feb-14
Cargo Insurance through the undersigned ☐ Not Covered ☐ Covered according to attached Policy	No. of Originals 0 (ZERO)	Stamp and Signature AS CARRIER
For delivery of goods please apply to: SCHUMACHER CARGO LOGISTICS LOS ANGELES CA 90248 UNITED STATES		

Standard Conditions (1992) governing the FIATA MULTIMODAL TRANSPORT BILL OF LADING

CONTINUATION PAGE

BILL OF LADING - FNET048201

Consignor	Consignee		
TAS SCREEN PRINTING EQUIPMENT PTY LTD AUSTRALIA			
Notify Party	**Goods Collected From**	**ETD**	02-Feb-14
SAME AS CONSIGNEE	MELBOURNE, AUSTRALIA		
	Goods Delivered To	**ETA**	01-Mar-14
	LOS ANGELES, UNITED STATES		
	Gross Weight	**Volume**	
	2811 KG	15.89 M3	
Phone : Fax:	**Package Quantity** 3 CRT (OUTER)		

As Agreed

EXPRESS WORLDWIDE WPX DHL

From: TAS INTERNATIONAL

MEL

To: TAS AMERICA

US-ELA-ELA

C

1 / 1

Contents: SCREEN PRINTING MACHINE PARTS.

WAYBILL 14 9078 7471

* ARCHIVE DOC * WPX DHL

MEL

EXPRESS WORLDWIDE

23.0 kgs

Date: 2014-10-17

1

Contents: SCREEN PRINTING MACHINE PARTS.

Consignor
TAS SCREEN PRINTING EQUIPMENT PTY LTD

BILL OF LADING

NOT NEGOTIABLE UNLESS CONSIGNED "TO ORDER"

Consigned to order of
INC.

Freightnet International
INTERNATIONAL FREIGHT FORWARDERS

Freightnet International (Vic) Pty Ltd
ABN: 54 889 546 787

Notify Address
TEL: +818 246 9330
FAX: +818 246 9333

	Place of Receipt MELBOURNE, AUSTRALIA
Ocean Vessel OOCL NORFOLK / 138	**Port of loading** MELBOURNE, AUSTRALIA
Port of discharge SINGAPORE	**Place of Delivery** LOS ANGELES, UNITED STATES

EXPRES_
Express Bill of Lading

Marks and Numbers	Number and Kind of Packages	Description of Goods	Gross Weight	Measurement
N/A	1	x 40GP CONTAINER 7 crate(s) 3 x NEW 'TAS' AUTOMATIC SCREEN PRINTING MACHINES & ACCESSORIES; MODEL: COMPACT CX-12 SERIAL NO.: 1315 & 1320 MODEL: COMPACT CX-10 SERIAL NO.: 1316 CIF TERMS.	8269 KG	43.01 M3

Container	Seals	Type	Weight	Volume	Packages	Mode
OOLU7980408	372414	40GP	8269 KG	43.01 M3	7 CRT	CY/CY*

CAN: ACJ6TFJT7   Consol Ref: C00038150

Total Packages: ONE CONTAINER(S)   *Shipper Load Count and Sealed

SHIPPED ON BOARD 22-Dec-14   according to the declaration of the consignor

Declaration of interest of the consignor in timely delivery (Clause 6.2.)

Declared value for ad valorem rate according to the declaration of the consignor (Clauses 7 and 8)

The goods and instructions are accepted and dealt with subject to the Standard Conditions printed overleaf.

Taken in charge in apparent good order and condition, unless otherwise noted herein, at the place of receipt for transport and delivery as mentioned above.

One of these Multimodal Transport Bills of Lading must be surrendered duly endorsed in exchange for the goods. In Witness whereof the original Multimodal Transport Bills of Lading and all of this tenor and date have been signed in the number stated below, one of which being accomplished the other(s) to be void.

Freight amount	Freight Payable at	Place and date of issue
FREIGHT PREPAID	MELBOURNE, AUSTRALIA	MELBOURNE, AUSTRALIA 22-Dec-14
Cargo Insurance through the undersigned ☐ Not Covered ☐ Covered according to attached Policy	**No. of Originals** 0 (ZERO)	**Stamp and Signature** AS CARRIER

For delivery of goods please apply to:
SCHUMACHER CARGO LOGISTICS
550 W. 135TH STREET
GARDENA, CA (TEL:+1 562 408 6677)
LOS ANGELES CA 90248
UNITED STATES

CONTINUATION PAGE

BILL OF LADING - FNET053719

Consignor	Consignee		
TAS SCREEN PRINTING EQUIPMENT PTY LTD [redacted] AUSTRALIA	[redacted] INC. DBA TAS AMERICA [redacted]		
Notify Party TEL: [redacted]	**Goods Collected From** MELBOURNE, AUSTRALIA	**ETD**	22-Dec-14
	Goods Delivered To LOS ANGELES, UNITED STATES	**ETA**	28-Jan-15
	Gross Weight 8269 KG	**Volume** 43.01 M3	
Phone: Fax:	**Package Quantity** 7 CRT (OUTER)		

As Agreed

2015 INTERNATIONAL TRADE

DATE	INVOICE	DOLLAR AMOUNT
02/27/15	2249	$122,250.00
03/03/15	2249	$122,250.00
03/19/15	2254	$61,000.00
03/25/15	12989	$944.00
05/04/15	13029	$1,893.00
05/08/15	13037	$969.80
05/20/15	13046	$208.36
05/27/15	23474	$1,680.00
06/23/15	13066	$3,367.10
06/23/15	13066	$350.00
06/29/15	13077	$713.50
06/29/15	13077	$250.00
07/24/15	13109	$6,308.50
07/24/15	13109	$450.00
TOTAL		**TOTAL**
14		$322,634.26

2015 INTERNATIONAL TRADE

DATE	INVOICE	DOLLAR AMOUNT
02/27/15	2249	$122,250.00
03/03/15	2249	$122,250.00
03/19/15	2254	$61,000.00
03/25/15	12989	$944.00
05/04/15	13029	$1,893.00
05/08/15	13037	$969.80
05/20/15	13046	$208.36
05/27/15	23474	$1,680.00
06/23/15	13066	$3,367.10
06/23/15	13066	$350.00
06/29/15	13077	$713.50
06/29/15	13077	$250.00
07/24/15	13109	$6,308.50
07/24/15	13109	$450.00
TOTAL		**TOTAL**
14		$322,634.26

2015
INVOICES

TAS INTERNATIONAL
TAS SCREEN PRINTING EQUIPMENT PTY LTD – A.B.N. 85 006 692 351
25 Kitchen Road, Dandenong South, 3175 Victoria, Australia
Telephone: (613) 9587 2600 Fax: (613) 9587 2789
www.tasinternational.com.au

COMMERCIAL INVOICE

INVOICE NO. :	2249
DATE:	27/02/2015
YOUR PO # :	375
CUSTOMER REF # :	20 DAYS

INVOICE TO:
[redacted] INC.
U.S.A
TEL: +818 246 9330 | FAX: +818 246 9333

SHIP TO:
[redacted] INC.
U.S.A
TEL: +818 246 9330 | FAX: +818 246 9333

DESCRIPTION OF GOODS AND/OR SERVICES	UNIT PRICE	QUANTITY	TOTAL
NEW 'TAS' AUTOMATIC SCREEN PRINTING MACHINES & ACCESSORIES;	$40,750.00	3	USD 122,250.00
MODEL : COMPACT CX-10			
SERIAL NO. : 1317, 1318 AND 1319			
INCLUDES STANDARD ACCESSORIES:-			
ADULT QUICK RELEASE PALLETS - 470MM X 610MM (18.5" X 24")		36	
SLEEVE QUICK RELEASE PALLETS - 127MM X 610MM (5" X 24")		12	
SQUEEGEES WITH RUBBER - 460MM (18")		30	
FIG7 FLOODBARS - 460MM (18")		30	
MACHINE PRINT AREA UPTO 18" X 20" | MAX SCREEN SIZE 24" X 30"			
MACHINE ELECTRICAL REQUIREMENTS: 220V / 3 PHASE			
AC ELECTRIC ROTATION AND PRINT HEADS			
CENTRAL OFF CONTACT & ROTO PRINT PROGRAM			
PNEUMATIC SCREEN CLAMPING AND INDIVIDUAL HEAD OFF CONTACT			
MULTI- FUNCTIONAL FOOT SWITCH & SKIP SHIRT PAUSE PEDAL			
FRONT, CENTRE AND REAR MICRO REGISTRATION			
MACHINE DIRECTION OF ROTATION: 1X CW & 2X ACW			
PACKING & CRATING			
FREIGHT TERMS : EX WORKS			
PAYMENT TERMS : 50% DEPOSIT ON ORDER. BALANCE TO BE PAID PRIOR TO SHIPMENT.			
MANUFACTURED IN VICTORIA, AUSTRALIA ***COUNTRY OF ORIGIN AUSTRALIA***	SUBTOTAL		USD 122,250.00
	TOTAL, EX WORKS		USD 122,250.00

Warranty Terms: Full warranty period (2yr) covers parts manufactured solely by TAS.. Commercially bought in parts (Motors, Gear Boxes, Inverters etc) are covered by the manufacturers standard 12 month warranty period only.

Beneficiary's Telegraphic Transfer Bank Account Details:
(Please note that all bank charges or fees outside of Australia are to be borne by customer)

Account Name: TAS SCREEN PRINTING EQUIPMENT PTY LTD
Account number: [redacted]
BSD Number: [redacted]

TAS INTERNATIONAL

TAS SCREEN PRINTING EQUIPMENT PTY LTD – A.B.N. 85 006 692 351

www.tasinternational.com.au

COMMERCIAL INVOICE

INVOICE NO. :	2249
DATE:	3/03/2015
YOUR PO # :	375
CUSTOMER REF # :	20 DAYS

INVOICE TO:

INC.

U.S.A

SHIP TO:

INC.

U.S.A

DESCRIPTION OF GOODS AND/OR SERVICES	UNIT PRICE	QUANTITY	TOTAL
NEW 'TAS' AUTOMATIC SCREEN PRINTING MACHINES & ACCESSORIES;	$40,750.00	3	USD 122,250.00
MODEL : COMPACT CX-10			
SERIAL NO. : 1317, 1318 AND 1319			
INCLUDES STANDARD ACCESSORIES:-			
ADULT QUICK RELEASE PALLETS - 470MM X 610MM (18.5" X 24")		36	
SLEEVE QUICK RELEASE PALLETS - 127MM X 610MM (5" X 24")		12	
SQUEEGEES WITH RUBBER - 460MM (18")		30	
FIG7 FLOODBARS - 460MM (18")		30	
MACHINE PRINT AREA UPTO 18" X 20" | MAX SCREEN SIZE 24" X 30"			
MACHINE ELECTRICAL REQUIREMENTS: 220V / 3 PHASE			
AC ELECTRIC ROTATION AND PRINT HEADS			
CENTRAL OFF CONTACT & ROTO PRINT PROGRAM			
PNEUMATIC SCREEN CLAMPING AND INDIVIDUAL HEAD OFF CONTACT			
MULTI- FUNCTIONAL FOOT SWITCH & SKIP SHIRT PAUSE PEDAL			
FRONT, CENTRE AND REAR MICRO REGISTRATION			
MACHINE DIRECTION OF ROTATION: 1X CW & 2X ACW			
PACKING & CRATING			
FREIGHT TERMS : EX WORKS			
PAYMENT TERMS : 50% DEPOSIT ON ORDER, BALANCE TO BE PAID PRIOR TO SHIPMENT.			
MANUFACTURED IN VICTORIA, AUSTRALIA ***COUNTRY OF ORIGIN AUSTRALIA***	SUBTOTAL		USD 122,250.00
	TOTAL, EX WORKS		USD 122,250.00

Warranty Terms: Full warranty period (2yr) covers parts manufactured solely by TAS. Commercially bought in parts (Motors, Gear Boxes, Inverters etc) are covered by the manufacturers standard 12 month warranty period only.

Beneficiary's Telegraphic Transfer Bank Account Details:

(Please note that all bank charges or fees outside of Australia are to be borne by customer)

Account Name: TAS SCREEN PRINTING EQUIPMENT PTY LTD

Account number:

TAS INTERNATIONAL
TAS SCREEN PRINTING EQUIPMENT PTY LTD – A.B.N. 85 006 692 351
www.tasinternational.com.au

COMMERCIAL INVOICE

INVOICE NO. :	2254
DATE:	19/03/2015
YOUR PO # :	394
CUSTOMER REF # :	Earth Sun Moon

INVOICE TO:
INC.

SHIP TO:
INC.

AND/OR SERVICES	UNIT PRICE	QUANTITY	TOTAL
1 X NEW 'TAS' AUTOMATIC SCREEN PRINTING MACHINE & ACCESSORIES;	$58,000.00	1	USD 58,000.00
MODEL : COMPACT CX-14			
SERIAL NO. : 1324			
INCLUDES STANDARD ACCESSORIES:			
SET OF (16) ADULT QUICK RELEASE PALLETS - 470MM X 610MM (18.5" X 24")			
SET OF (14) SQUEEGEES WITH RUBBER - 460MM (18")			
SET OF (14) FIG7 FLOODBARS - 460MM (18")			
MACHINE PRINT AREA UPTO 18" X 20" | MAX SCREEN SIZE 24" X 30"			
MACHINE ELECTRICAL REQUIREMENTS: 220V / 3 PHASE			
MACHINE DIRECTION OF ROTATION: ACW ROTATION			
AC ELECTRIC ROTATION AND PRINT HEADS			
CENTRAL OFF CONTACT & ROTO PRINT PROGRAM			
PNEUMATIC SCREEN CLAMPING AND INDIVIDUAL HEAD OFF CONTACT			
MULTI- FUNCTIONAL FOOT SWITCH SKIP SHIRT PAUSE PEDAL			
FRONT, CENTRE AND REAR MICRO REGISTRATION			
PACKING & CRATING			
FREIGHT TERMS : FREIGHT PREPAID - CIF LONG BEACH PORT			
PAYMENT TERMS : 50% DEPOSIT ON ORDER. BALANCE TO BE PAID PRIOR TO SHIPMENT.			

MANUFACTURED IN VICTORIA, AUSTRALIA ***COUNTRY OF ORIGIN AUSTRALIA***

SUBTOTAL EXW	USD 58,000.00
FREIGHT + INSURANCE	USD 3,000.00
TOTAL, CIF LONG BEACH	USD 61,000.00

Warranty Terms: Full warranty period (2yr) covers parts manufactured solely by TAS.. Commercially bought in parts (Motors, Gear Boxes, Inverters etc) are covered by the manufacturers standard 12 month warranty period only.

Beneficiary's Telegraphic Transfer Bank Account Details:
(Please note that all bank charges or fees outside of Australia are to be borne by customer)

Account Name: TAS SCREEN PRINTING EQUIPMENT PTY LTD
Account number:

TAS International

TAS SCREEN PRINTING EQUIPMENT PTY LTD

Phone:

ABN:

Tax Invoice No. 12989

Page 1 of 1

Invoice Address: TAS AMERICA
U.S.A.
Phone: +
Fax:

Shipping Address: TAS AMERICA
U.S.A.
Phone:

Ship Via	Tracking Number	Despatch Date	Shipment No	Picking/Pro Inv. No
DHL Express	2357323382	25/03/2015	12447	12964

Invoice Date	Due Date	Payment Terms	Your Order	Salesperson
25/03/2015	24/04/2015	30 Days W/Discount	Mel	Malcolm Cowen

Part ID / Description:	Order Qty:	U/M:	Unit Price:	Unit Discount:	Extended Price:
205RA-02-20-0JT Crank Arm 205Ra/Roc & 203El	1.00	EA	295.00	88.50	USD$206.50
205RA-02-11 Indexer Slotted Plate	1.00	EA	350.00	105.00	USD$245.00
200RA-05-00-30 Spring Clip Quick Release (Complete)	20.00	EA	23.75	7.13	USD$332.50
SALES Micro Reg. Sticker	50.00	EA	0.50	0.15	USD$17.50
SALES AIR LOG STICKER	50.00	EA	0.50	0.15	USD$17.50

Incorrect part # 205RA-02-20-0JT correct part is 205RA-02- 15 this was sent out to Mel..

ON BACK ORDER - Print Stroke Adjustment Sticker*

COUNTRY OF ORIGIN - AUSTRALIA

PAYMENT BY T/T - Account Details are:
Account Name: TAS SCREEN PRINTING EQUIPMENT PTY LTD
Account Number:
Swift Code:
Bank Name: ANZ BANK
Branch Address:
BY CREDIT CARD - VISA or MASTER - Please send us your card details

Invoice Sub-total	USD$819.00
Freight	USD$125.00
INVOICE TOTAL	**USD$944.00**

TAS International

Tax Invoice No. 13029

Invoice Address: TAS AMERICA

Shipping Address: TAS AMERICA

Ship Via	Tracking Number	Despatch Date		
Other...	---	4/05/2015		

Invoice Date	Due Date	Payment Terms	Your Order	Salesperson
4/05/2015	4/05/2015	C.O.D.	Malcolm	

Part ID / Description:	Order Qty:	U/M:	Unit Price:	Unit Discount:	Extended Price:
TRAVEL Airfare From Melbourne to LA for Malcolm	1.00	EA	1,893.49	0.00	AU$1,893.49

COUNTRY OF ORIGIN - AUSTRALIA

PAYMENT BY T/T - Account Details are:

Account Name:	TAS SCREEN PRINTING EQUIPMENT PTY LTD
Account Number:	395814USD00001
Swift Code:	ANZBAU3M
BSB Number:	013024
Bank Name:	ANZ BANK
Branch Address:	100 Queen St. Melbourne, VIC, 3000, Australia

BY CREDIT CARD - VISA or MASTER - Please send us your card details

Invoice Sub-total	AU$1,893.49
Freight	AU$0.00
INVOICE TOTAL	**AU$1,893.49**

2015 AIR BILLS OR SHIPPING INVOICES

Consignor
TAS SCREEN PRINTING EQUIPMENT PTY LTD
25 KITCHEN ROAD
DANDENONG SOUTH VIC 3175
AUSTRALIA

HBL FNET055628 Country Code AU

BILL OF LADING
NOT NEGOTIABLE UNLESS CONSIGNED "TO ORDER"

Consigned to order of
MAY NATIONAL, INC.
DBA TAS AMERICA
818 ALLEN AVENUE
GLENDALE CA 91201
UNITED STATES

Freightnet International
INTERNATIONAL FREIGHT FORWARDERS

Notify Address
TEL: +818 246 9330
FAX: +818 246 9333

	Place of Receipt MELBOURNE, AUSTRALIA
Ocean Vessel CAP CAPRICORN / 420N	**Port of loading** MELBOURNE, AUSTRALIA
Port of discharge LONG BEACH, UNITED STATES	**Place of Delivery** LONG BEACH, UNITED STATES

Fax: +61-3-9335 2482
E-mail: mail@freightnetvic.com.au

EXPRESS
Express Bill of Lading

Marks and Numbers	Number and Kind of Packages	Description of Goods	Gross Weight	Measurement
N/A		1 x 20GP CONTAINER 3 Crate(s) 1 x NEW 'TAS' AUTOMATIC SCREEN PRINTING MACHINE & ACCESSORIES; MODEL: COMPACT CX-14 SERIAL NO.: 1324 CIF LONG BEACH	3775 KG	18.57 M3

Container	Seals	Type	Weight	Volume	Packages	Mode
CAXU6513792	100518	20GP	3775 KG	18.57 M3	3 CRT	CY/CY*

CAN: ACKWP3A3C   Consol Ref: C00039255
Total Packages: ONE CONTAINER(S)   *Shipper Load Count and Sealed
SHIPPED ON BOARD 24-Mar-15   according to the declaration of the consignor

Declaration of interest of the consignor in timely delivery (Clause 6.2.)

Declared value for ad valorem rate according to the declaration of the consignor (Clauses 7 and 8)

The goods and instructions are accepted and dealt with subject to the Standard Conditions printed overleaf.

Taken in charge in apparent good order and condition, unless otherwise noted herein, at the place of receipt for transport and delivery as mentioned above.

One of these Multimodal Transport Bills of Lading must be surrendered duly endorsed in exchange for the goods. In Witness whereof the original Multimodal Transport Bills of Lading and all of this tenor and date have been signed in the number stated below, one of which being accomplished the other(s) to be void.

Freight amount FREIGHT PREPAID	**Freight Payable at** MELBOURNE, AUSTRALIA	**Place and date of issue** MELBOURNE, AUSTRALIA 24-Mar-15
Cargo Insurance through the undersigned ☐ Not Covered ☐ Covered according to attached Policy	**No. of Originals** 0 (ZERO)	**Stamp and Signature** AS CARRIER

Standard Conditions (1992) governing the FIATA MULTIMODAL TRANSPORT BILL OF LADING

Definitions

- "Freight Forwarder" means the Multimodal Transport Operator who issues this FBL and is named on the face of it and assumes liability for the performance of the multimodal transport contract as a carrier.
- "Merchant" means and includes the Shipper, the Consignor, the Consignee, the Holder of this FBL, the Receiver and the Owner of the Goods.
- "Consignor" means the person who concludes the multimodal transport contract with the Freight Forwarder.
- "Consignee" means the person entitled to receive the goods from the Freight Forwarder.
- "Taken in charge" means that the goods have been handed over to and accepted for carriage by the Freight Forwarder at the place of receipt evidenced in this FBL.
- "Goods" means any property including live animals as well as containers, pallets or similar articles of transport or packaging not supplied by the Freight Forwarder, irrespective of whether such property is to be or is carried on or under deck.

1. **Applicability**

   Notwithstanding the heading "FIATA Multimodal Transport Bill of Lading (FBL)" these conditions shall also apply if only one mode of transport is used.

2. **Issuance of this FBL**

   2.1. By issuance of this FBL the Freight Forwarder:

   2.1.1. undertakes to perform and/or in his own name to procure the performance of the entire transport, from the place at which the goods are taken in charge (place of receipt evidenced in this FBL) to the place of delivery designated in this FBL;

[illegible]

CONTINUATION PAGE

BILL OF LADING - FNET055628

Consignor	Consignee		
TAS SCREEN PRINTING EQUIPMENT PTY LTD AUSTRALIA	INC. DBA TAS AMERICA UNITED STATES		
Notify Party TEL: +	**Goods Collected From** MELBOURNE, AUSTRALIA	**ETD**	23-Mar-15
	Goods Delivered To	**ETA**	17-Apr-15
	Gross Weight 3775 KG	**Volume** 18.57 M3	
Phone: Fax:	**Package Quantity** 3 CRT (OUTER)		

As Agreed

SCHUMACHER
CARGO LOGISTICS
Confidence in Transport.

www.sclusa.com

Invoice Number	Currency
74135	USD
Date	Due Date
05/01/2015	05/31/2015

Bill To
TAS AMERICA — Terms: 30

Shipper
TAS SCREEN PRINTING EQUIPMENT PTY LTD
Australia
Phone:

Shipment #: MEL0033927
Origin: MELBOURNE
Destination: LONG BEACH
Final Destination: LONG BEACH
Carrier: ANL CONTAINER LINE PTY LIMITED
Vessel: CAP CAPRICORN
Voyage: 1700SANL
Departure: 03/30/2015
Arrival: 04/22/2015

Consignee
TAS AMERICA
UNITED STATES
Phone:

Code	Description	Qty	Unit	Rate	Amount
ISF	ISF CHARGE	1.00	EACH	25.000	25.00
CST	CUSTOMS CLEARANCE	1.00	EACH	175.000	175.00
THC	TERMINAL HANDLING CHARGES	1.00	EACH	580.000	580.00
TAX	TAX (CLIENT)	1.00	EACH	72.500	72.50
BND	BOND (US CUSTOMS)	1.00	EACH	261.000	261.00
PIER	PIER PASS	1.00	EACH	125.000	125.00
CTF	CLEAN TRUCK FEE (LOS ANGLES)	1.00	EACH	70.000	70.00
ILF	INLAND FREIGHT	1.00	EACH	450.000	450.00
FSC	FUEL SURCHARGE	1.00	EACH	45.000	45.00
				TOTAL USD	1,803.50

Comments : 20FT CONTAINER CAXU6513792

DEAR VALUED CLIENT, PAYMENT TERMS ARE AS FOLLOWS:
INVOICES SHOULD BE PAID AS SOON AS RECEIVED. FAILURE TO PAY ON OR BEFORE DEPARTURE DATE CAN CAUSE LATE FEES AT 5% PER MONTH AND ASSOCIATED STORAGE COSTS. VEHICLES RECEIVED WITHOUT COMPLETE DOCUMENTATION WILL INCURR $10.00 PER DAY DELAY/STORAGE CHARGES.

PAYMENT OPTIONS - WIRE TRANSFER - PERSONAL OR COMPANY CHECK ($10.00 RETURN CHECK FEE) - CASH.

CARD PAYMENTS ARE ACCEPTED ONLINE AT: WWW.SCLUSA.COM
SERVICE/HANDLING FEES APPLY.

Electronic Funds Transfer

Please reference invoice # on the payment

FOR WIRE TRANSFERS

BENEFICIARY NAME:	SCHUMACHER CARGO LOGISTICS, INC.
BENEFICIARY ACCOUNT NO:	050007166207220
ROUTING NO.	121000248
SWIFT CODE:	WFBIUS6S
BANK NAME:	WELLS FARGO BANK, N.A.
BANK ADDRESS:	420 MONTGOMERY SAN FRANCISCO, CA 94104

Invoice Number	74135
Customer Name	TAS AMERICA
Amount Due $	1,803.50
Invoices Date	05/01/2015

Please make your check payable to:

SCHUMACHER CARGO LOGISTICS, INC.

MAIL PAYMENTS TO:
SCHUMACHER CARGO LOGISTICS, INC
ACCOUNTS RECEIVABLE
550 WEST 135TH STREET, GARDENA, CA 90248 - USA
OR FAX TO AIR FAX: 424 233-1008

PAYMENT IS DUE AS PER YOUR INVOICE TERMS
FAILURE TO PAY ON OR BEFORE DUE DATE, CAN CAUSE DELAYED DEPARTURES WITH ADDITIONAL LATE FEES AT 5% PER MONTH AND ASSOCIATED STORAGE COSTS
OUR SERVICE TERMS & CONDITIONS ARE AVAILABLE ON OUR WEB SITE AT: WWW.SCLUSA.COM.

WHEN YOU PROVIDE A CHECK AS PAYMENT, YOU AUTHORIZE US EITHER TO USE INFORMATION FROM YOUR CHECK TO MAKE A ONE-TIME ELECTRONIC FUND TRANSFER FROM YOUR ACCOUNT OR TO PROCESS THE PAYMENT AS A CHECK TRANSACTION.

WE LOOK FORWARD TO SERVICING YOUR FUTURE SHIPMENTS.

From: 013 9587 2600 Origin ID: MELA

MS. HIROS AZID
TAS SCREEN PRINTING EQUIPMENT PA.
25 KITCHEN ROAD
ABN: 05 006 692 351
DANDENONG SOUTH VIC, 3175
AUSTRALIA

FedEx Express

E

SHIP TO: (818) 246-9330 BILL SENDER

MEL ■
TAS AMARICA, INC.
1425 FIRST STREET

SAN FERNANDO, CA 91340
US

Ship Date: 23JUN15
ActWgt: 7.0 KG MAN Dims: 30 X 30 X 20 CM
CAD: 0053707/GSMW0670

REF: inv.13066
DESC-1: SCREEN PRINTING EQUIPMENT / MACHINE PARTS
DESC-2:
DESC-3:
DESC-4:

COUNTRY MFG: AU
CARRIAGE VALUE: 0.00 USD
CUSTOMS VALUE: 350.00 USD
T/C: S 169756465 D/T: R
SIGN: MS. HIROS AZID
EIN/VAT:
PKG TYPE: CUSTOMER

AA
INTL ECONOMY
ISR
91340
CA-US
BUR

TRK# 6325 5568 3987
0430

SH AHCA

518C1/6705/FR03

The Warsaw Convention may apply and will govern and in most cases limit the liability of Federal Express for loss or delay of or damage to your shipment. Subject to the conditions of the contract.

CONSIGNEE COPY - PLEASE PLACE IN POUCH

CONSIGNEE COPY – PLEASE PLACE IN POUCH

PLEASE FOLD THIS SHIPPING DOCUMENT IN HALF AND PLACE IT IN A WAYBILL POUCH AFFIXED TO YOUR SHIPMENT SO THAT THE BARCODE PORTION OF THE LABEL CAN BE READ AND SCANNED. **WARNING: USE ONLY THE PRINTED ORIGINAL LABEL FOR SHIPPING. USING PHOTOCOPY OF THIS LABEL FOR SHIPPING IS FRAUDULENT AND COULD RESULT IN ADDITIONAL BILLING CHARGES, ALONG WITH THE CANCELLATION OF YOUR FEDEX ACCOUNT NUMBER.

From: 613 9587 2600 Origin ID: MELA FedEx. Express
MS. HIROS AZID
TAS SCREEN PRINTING EQUIPMENT P/L
25 KITCHEN ROAD
ABN: 55 006602 351
DANDENONG SOUTH VIC, 3175
AUSTRALIA

SHIP TO: (818) 246-9330 BILL SENDER

SAN FERNANDO, CA 91340
US

Ship Date: 29JUN15
ActWgt: 10.1 KG MAN
CAD: 6053707/GSMW0670
Dims: 30 X 19 X 19 CM

REF: INV 13077
DESC-1: SCREEN PRINTING EQUIPMENT / MACHINE PARTS - BELLCRANK
DESC-2:
DESC-3:
DESC-4:

T/C: S 109756165 D/T: R
SIGN: MS. HIROS AZID
EIN/VAT:
PKG TYPE: CUSTOMER

AA
INTL ECONOMY

TRK# 6325 5568 4045
0430

ISR
91340
CA-US
BUR

SH AHCA

CONSIGNEE COPY - PLEASE PLACE IN POUCH

CONSIGNEE COPY – PLEASE PLACE IN POUCH

PLEASE FOLD THIS SHIPPING DOCUMENT IN HALF AND PLACE IT IN A WAYBILL POUCH AFFIXED TO YOUR SHIPMENT SO THAT THE BARCODE PORTION OF THE LABEL CAN BE READ AND SCANNED. **WARNING: USE ONLY THE PRINTED ORIGINAL LABEL FOR SHIPPING. USING PHOTOCOPY OF THIS LABEL FOR SHIPPING IS FRAUDULENT AND COULD RESULT IN ADDITIONAL BILLING CHARGES, ALONG WITH THE CANCELLATION OF YOUR FEDEX ACCOUNT NUMBER.

EXPRESS WORLDWIDE **WPX** DHL

WSI 3.14.0 / "90-1411"

From :

Australia

Origin:

MEL

Contact: Ph : 61395872000

To : TAS AMERICA

1

1425 First Street

US-VNY-VNY

C

Day Time

Ref:INV.13109

Date: 24-Jul-2015

Pce/Shpt Weight 27.60/27.6 kgs

Piece 1 / 1

Contents:SCREEN PRINTING EQUIPMENT/MACHINE PARTS. HS Code: 84439100;

WAYBILL 99 8694 6830

(2L)US91340+48000001

(J) JD01 4600 0021 0926 8053

2013 INCOME TAX RETURN

Form **1120S** — **U.S. Income Tax Return for an S Corporation** — OMB No. 1545-0130 — **2013**

Department of the Treasury, Internal Revenue Service

► Do not file this form unless the corporation has filed or is attaching Form 2553 to elect to be an S corporation.
► Information about Form 1120S and its separate instructions is at *www.irs.gov/form1120s*.

For calendar year 2013 or tax year beginning , 2013, ending ,

A S election effective date: 2/13/2009	TYPE OR PRINT: [redacted] INC	D Employer identification number: [redacted]
B Business activity code number (see instrs): 423800	[redacted]	E Date incorporated: 2/19/2009
C Check if Schedule M-3 attached ☐	[redacted] 2	F Total assets (see instructions): $ 295,076.

G Is the corporation electing to be an S corporation beginning with this tax year? ☐ Yes ☒ No If 'Yes,' attach Form 2553 if not already filed

H Check if: (1) ☐ Final return (2) ☐ Name change (3) ☒ Address change (4) ☐ Amended return (5) ☐ S election termination or revocation

I Enter the number of shareholders who were shareholders during any part of the tax year ► 1

Caution. Include **only** trade or business income and expenses on lines 1a through 21. See the instructions for more information.

Section	Line	Description				Amount
INCOME	1a	Gross receipts or sales	1a	445,511.		
	b	Returns and allowances	1b			
	c	Balance. Subtract line 1b from line 1a			1c	445,511.
	2	Cost of goods sold (attach Form 1125-A)			2	159,172.
	3	Gross profit. Subtract line 2 from line 1c			3	286,339.
	4	Net gain (loss) from Form 4797, line 17 (attach Form 4797)			4	
	5	Other income (loss) (see instrs — att statement) SEE STATEMENT 1			5	6,026.
	6	**Total income (loss).** Add lines 3 through 5 ►			6	292,365.
DEDUCTIONS (SEE INSTRS)	7	Compensation of officers (see instructions - attach Form 1125-E)			7	39,370.
	8	Salaries and wages (less employment credits)			8	39,370.
	9	Repairs and maintenance			9	4,077.
	10	Bad debts			10	
	11	Rents			11	57,038.
	12	Taxes and licenses			12	17,194.
	13	Interest			13	7,664.
	14	Depreciation not claimed on Form 1125-A or elsewhere on return (attach Form 4562)			14	5,728.
	15	Depletion **(Do not deduct oil and gas depletion.)**			15	
	16	Advertising			16	1,838.
	17	Pension, profit-sharing, etc, plans			17	
	18	Employee benefit programs			18	1,104.
	19	Other deductions (attach statement) SEE STATEMENT 2			19	109,246.
	20	**Total deductions.** Add lines 7 through 19 ►			20	282,629.
	21	**Ordinary business income (loss).** Subtract line 20 from line 6			21	9,736.
TAX AND PAYMENTS	22a	Excess net passive income or LIFO recapture tax *(see instructions)*	22a			
	b	Tax from Schedule D (Form 1120S)	22b			
	c	Add lines 22a and 22b (see instructions for additional taxes)			22c	
	23a	2013 estimated tax payments and 2012 overpayment credited to 2013	23a			
	b	Tax deposited with Form 7004	23b			
	c	Credit for federal tax paid on fuels (attach Form 4136)	23c			
	d	Add lines 23a through 23c			23d	
	24	Estimated tax penalty (see instructions). Check if Form 2220 is attached ► ☐			24	
	25	Amount owed. If line 23d is smaller than the total of lines 22c and 24, enter amount owed			25	0.
	26	**Overpayment.** If line 23d is larger than the total of lines 22c and 24, enter amount overpaid			26	
	27	Enter amount from line 26 **Credited to 2014 estimated tax** ►	Refunded ►		27	

Sign Here — Under penalties of perjury, I declare that I have examined this return, including accompanying schedules and statements, and to the best of my knowledge and belief, it is true, correct, and complete. Declaration of preparer (other than taxpayer) is based on all information of which preparer has any knowledge.

► Signature of officer — Date — ► PRESIDENT & CEO (Title)

May the IRS discuss this return with the preparer shown below (see instructions)? ☒ Yes ☐ No

Paid Preparer Use Only

Print/Type preparer's name	Preparer's signature	Date	Check ☐ if self-employed	PTIN
[redacted]	[redacted]			[redacted]
Firm's name ► [redacted] C			Firm's EIN ►	
Firm's address ► [redacted]			Phone no. [redacted]	

BAA For Paperwork Reduction Act Notice, see separate instructions. SPSA0105L 06/28/13

Schedule B | Other Information (see instructions)

		Yes	No
1	Check accounting method: a [ ] Cash b [X] Accrual c [ ] Other (specify) ►		
2	See the instructions and enter the: a Business activity ► SALES b Product or service ► SERVICE		
3	At any time during the tax year, was any shareholder of the corporation a disregarded entity, a trust, an estate, or a nominee or similar person? If "Yes," attach Schedule B-1, Information on Certain Shareholders of an S Corporation		X
4a	At the end of the tax year, did the corporation: Own directly 20% or more, or own, directly or indirectly, 50% or more of the total stock issued and outstanding of any foreign or domestic corporation? For rules of constructive ownership, see instructions. If 'Yes,' complete (i) through (v) below		X

(i) Name of Corporation	(ii) Employer Identification Number (if any)	(iii) Country of Incorporation	(iv) Percentage of Stock Owned	(v) If Percentage in (iv) is 100%, Enter the Date (if any) a Qualified Subchapter S Subsidiary Election Was Made

		Yes	No
b	Own directly an interest of 20% or more, or own, directly or indirectly, an interest of 50% or more in the profit, loss, or capital in any foreign or domestic partnership (including an entity treated as a partnership) or in the beneficial interest of a trust? For rules of constructive ownership, see instructions. If 'Yes,' complete (i) through (v) below		X

(i) Name of Entity	(ii) Employer Identification Number (if any)	(iii) Type of Entity	(iv) Country of Organization	(v) Maximum % Owned in Profit, Loss, or Capital

		Yes	No
5a	At the end of the tax year, did the corporation have any outstanding shares of restricted stock?		X
	If 'Yes,' complete lines (i) and (ii) below. (i) Total shares of restricted stock ► (ii) Total shares of non-restricted stock ►		
b	At the end of the tax year, did the corporation have any outstanding stock options, warrants, or similar instruments?		X
	If 'Yes,' complete lines (i) and (ii) below. (i) Total shares of stock outstanding at the end of the tax year ► (ii) Total shares of stock oustanding if all instruments were executed ►		
6	Has this corporation filed, or is it required to file, Form 8918, Material Advisor Disclosure Statement, to provide information on any reportable transaction?		X
7	Check this box if the corpor[redacted]n issued publicly offered debt instruments with original issue discount ► [ ] If checked, the corporation [redacted] have to file Form 8281, Information Return for Publicly Offered Original Issue Discount Instruments.		
8	If the corporation: (a) was a C corporation before it elected to be an S corporation or the corporation acquired an asset with a basis determined by reference to the basis of the asset (or the basis of any other property) in the hands of a C corporation and (b) has net unrealized built-in gain in excess of the net recognized built-in gain from prior years, enter the net unrealized built-in gain reduced by net recognized built-in gain from prior years (see instructions) ►$		
9	Enter the accumulated earnings and profits of the corporation at the end of the tax year $		
10	Does the corporation satisfy both of the following conditions?		
a	The corporation's total receipts (see instructions) for the tax year were less than $250,000		
b	The corporation's total assets at the end of the tax year were less than $250,000		X
	If 'Yes,' the corporation is not required to complete Schedules L and M-1.		
11	During the tax year, did the corporation have any non-shareholder debt that was canceled, was forgiven, or had the terms modified so as to reduce the principal amount of the debt?		X
	If 'Yes,' enter the amount of principal reduction $		
12	During the tax year, was a qualified subchapter S subsidiary election terminated or revoked? If 'Yes', see instructions		X
13a	Did the corporation make any payments in 2013 that would require it to file Form(s) 1099?	X	
b	If 'Yes,' did the corporation file or will it file required Forms 1099?	X	

Form 1120S (2013)

Schedule K Shareholders' Pro Rata Share Items

	Item	Line	Total amount
Income (Loss)	1 Ordinary business income (loss) (page 1, line 21)	1	9,736.
	2 Net rental real estate income (loss) (attach Form 8825)	2	
	3a Other gross rental income (loss) — 3a		
	b Expenses from other rental activities (attach statement) — 3b		
	c Other net rental income (loss). Subtract line 3b from line 3a	3c	
	4 Interest income	4	
	5 Dividends: a Ordinary dividends	5a	
	b Qualified dividends — 5b		
	6 Royalties	6	
	7 Net short-term capital gain (loss) (attach Schedule D (Form 1120S))	7	
	8a Net long-term capital gain (loss) (attach Schedule D (Form 1120S))	8a	
	b Collectibles (28%) gain (loss) — 8b		
	c Unrecaptured section 1250 gain (attach statement) — 8c		
	9 Net section 1231 gain (loss) (attach Form 4797)	9	
	10 Other income (loss) (see instructions) Type ▶	10	
Deductions	11 Section 179 deduction (attach Form 4562)	11	
	12a Charitable contributions	12a	
	b Investment interest expense	12b	
	c Section 59(e)(2) expenditures (1) Type ▶ (2) Amount ▶	12c (2)	
	d Other deductions (see instructions) Type ▶	12d	
Credits	13a Low-income housing credit (section 42(j)(5))	13a	
	b Low-income housing credit (other)	13b	
	c Qualified rehabilitation expenditures (rental real estate) (attach Form 3468)	13c	
	d Other rental real estate credits (see instrs) Type ▶	13d	
	e Other rental credits (see instrs) Type ▶	13e	
	f Biofuel producer credit (attach Form 6478)	13f	
	g Other credits (see instructions) Type ▶	13g	
Foreign Transactions	14a Name of country or U.S. possession ▶		
	b Gross income from all sources	14b	
	c Gross income sourced at shareholder level	14c	
	Foreign gross income sourced at corporate level		
	d Passive category	14d	
	e General category	14e	
	f Other (attach statement)	14f	
	Deductions allocated and apportioned at shareholder level		
	g Interest expense	14g	
	h Other	14h	
	Deductions allocated and apportioned at corporate level to foreign source income		
	i Passive category	14i	
	j General category	14j	
	k Other (attach statement)	14k	
	Other information		
	l Total foreign taxes (check one): ▶ ☐ Paid ☐ Accrued	14l	
	m Reduction in taxes available for credit (attach statement)	14m	
	n Other foreign tax information (attach statement)		
Alternative Minimum Tax (AMT) Items	15a Post-1986 depreciation adjustment	15a	
	b Adjusted gain or loss	15b	
	c Depletion (other than oil and gas)	15c	
	d Oil, gas, and geothermal properties – gross income	15d	
	e Oil, gas, and geothermal properties – deductions	15e	
	f Other AMT items (attach statement)	15f	
Items Affecting Shareholder Basis	16a Tax-exempt interest income	16a	
	b Other tax-exempt income	16b	
	c Nondeductible expenses	16c	427.
	d Distributions (attach stmt if required) (see instrs)	16d	

Schedule K | Shareholders' Pro Rata Share Items (continued)

			Total amount
Other Information	17a Investment income	17a	
	b Investment expenses	17b	
	c Dividend distributions paid from accumulated earnings and profits	17c	
	d Other items and amounts (attach statement)		
Reconciliation	18 **Income/loss reconciliation.** Combine the amounts on lines 1 through 10 in the far right column. From the result, subtract the sum of the amounts on lines 11 through 12d and lines 14l	18	9,736.

Schedule L | Balance Sheets per Books

Assets	Beginning of tax year (a)	(b)	End of tax year (c)	(d)
1 Cash		2,227.		39,246.
2a Trade notes and accounts receivable	181,223.		28,229.	
b Less allowance for bad debts		181,223.		28,229.
3 Inventories		163,262.		147,631.
4 U.S. government obligations				
5 Tax-exempt securities (see instructions)				
6 Other current assets (attach stmt) SEE ST 3		72,245.		75,675.
7 Loans to shareholders				
8 Mortgage and real estate loans				
9 Other investments (attach statement)				
10a Buildings and other depreciable assets	1,722.		11,745.	
b Less accumulated depreciation	1,722.		7,450.	4,295.
11a Depletable assets				
b Less accumulated depletion				
12 Land (net of any amortization)				
13a Intangible assets (amortizable only)				
b Less accumulated amortization				
14 Other assets (attach stmt)				
15 Total assets		418,957.		295,076.
Liabilities and Shareholders' Equity				
16 Accounts payable		141,526.		25,021.
17 Mortgages, notes, bonds payable in less than 1 year				
18 Other current liabilities (attach stmt) SEE ST 4		138,079.		188,589.
19 Loans from shareholders				
20 Mortgages, notes, bonds payable in 1 year or more		67,195.		
21 Other liabilities (attach statement)				
22 Capital stock		5,000.		5,000.
23 Additional paid-in capital				
24 Retained earnings		67,157.		76,466.
25 Adjustments to shareholders' equity (att stmt)				
26 Less cost of treasury stock				
27 Total liabilities and shareholders' equity		418,957.		295,076.

SPSA0134L 05/29/13 Form 1120S (2013)

[redacted] With Income (Loss) per Return

Note: Schedule M-3 required instead of Schedule M-1 if total assets are $10 million or more – see instructions

1 Net income (loss) per books	9,309.	5 Income recorded on books this year not included on Schedule K, lines 1 through 10 (itemize): a Tax-exempt interest. $	
2 Income included on Schedule K, lines 1, 2, 3c, 4, 5a, 6, 7, 8a, 9, and 10, not recorded on books this year (itemize):			
3 Expenses recorded on books this year not included on Schedule K, lines 1 through 12, and 14l (itemize): a Depreciation $ b Travel and entertainment. $ SEE STATEMENT 5 427.	427.	6 Deductions included on Schedule K, lines 1 through 12, and 14l, not charged against book income this year (itemize): a Depreciation $	
		7 Add lines 5 and 6	0.
4 Add lines 1 through 3	9,736.	8 Income (loss) (Schedule K, ln 18). Ln 4 less ln 7	9,736.

Schedule M-2 **Analysis of Accumulated Adjustments Account, Other Adjustments Account, and Shareholders' Undistributed Taxable Income Previously Taxed** (see instructions)

	(a) Accumulated adjustments account	(b) Other adjustments account	(c) Shareholders' undistributed taxable income previously taxed
1 Balance at beginning of tax year	67,157.		
2 Ordinary income from page 1, line 21	9,736.		
3 Other additions			
4 Loss from page 1, line 21			
5 Other reductions SEE STATEMENT 6	(427.)		
6 Combine lines 1 through 5	76,466.		
7 Distributions other than dividend distributions			
8 Balance at end of tax year. Subtract line 7 from line 6	76,466.		

SPSA0134L 06/27/13 Form 1120S (2013)

Form **1125-A** (Rev December 2012) Department of the Treasury Internal Revenue Service

Cost of Goods Sold

▸ Attach to Form 1120, 1120-C, 1120-F, 1120-S, 1065, or 1065-B.
▸ Information about Form 1125-A and its instructions is at *www.irs.gov/form1125a*.

OMB No. 1545-2225

Name: [redacted] [redacted] INC | Employer identification number: [redacted]

1	Inventory at beginning of year	1	163,262.
2	Purchases	2	90,326.
3	Cost of labor	3	25,220.
4	Additional section 263A costs (attach schedule)	4	
5	Other costs (attach schedule) SEE STATEMENT 7	5	27,995.
6	**Total.** Add lines 1 through 5	6	306,803.
7	Inventory at end of year	7	147,631.
8	**Cost of goods sold.** Subtract line 7 from line 6. Enter here and on Form 1120, page 1, line 2 or the appropriate line of your tax return (see instructions)	8	159,172.

9 a Check all methods used for valuing closing inventory:
- (i) [X] Cost
- (ii) [ ] Lower of cost or market
- (iii) [ ] Other (Specify method used and attach explanation) ▸

b Check if there was a writedown of subnormal goods ▸ [ ]

c Check if the LIFO inventory method was adopted this tax year for any goods (if checked, attach Form 970) ▸ [ ]

d If the LIFO inventory method was used for this tax year, enter amount of closing inventory computed under LIFO | 9d |

e If property is produced or acquired for resale, do the rules of section 263A apply to the entity (see instructions)? [ ] Yes [X] No

f Was there any change in determining quantities, cost, or valuations between opening and closing inventory? If 'Yes,' attach explanation [ ] Yes [X] No

BAA For Paperwork Reduction Act Notice, see instructions. Form 1125-A (Rev 12-2012)

671113

☐ Final K-1 ☐ Amended K-1 OMB No. 1545-0130

Schedule K-1 (Form 1120S) **2013**

Department of the Treasury Internal Revenue Service

For calendar year 2013, or tax year beginning ________, 2013 ending ________

Shareholder's Share of Income, Deductions, Credits, etc

► See page 2 of form and separate instructions.

Part I Information About the Corporation

A Corporation's employer identification number

B Corporation's name, address, city, state, and ZIP code

[redacted] INC

C IRS Center where corporation filed return

E-FILE

Part II Information About the Shareholder

D Shareholder's identifying number

602-75-0616

E Shareholder's name, address, city, state, and ZIP code

F Shareholder's percentage of stock ownership for tax year 100 %

FOR IRS USE ONLY

Part III Shareholder's Share of Current Year Income, Deductions, Credits, and Other Items

1	Ordinary business income (loss) 9,736.	13	Credits
2	Net rental real estate income (loss)		
3	Other net rental income (loss)		
4	Interest income		
5a	[redacted]		
5b	Qualified dividends	14	Foreign transactions
6	Royalties		
7	Net short-term capital gain (loss)		
8a	Net long-term capital gain (loss)		
8b	Collectibles (28%) gain (loss)		
8c	Unrecaptured section 1250 gain		
9	Net section 1231 gain (loss)		
10	Other income (loss)	15	Alternative minimum tax (AMT) items
11	Section 179 deduction	16	Items affecting shareholder basis C 427.
12	Other deductions		
		17	Other information

*See attached statement for additional information.

BAA For Paperwork Reduction Act Notice, see Instructions for Form 1120S. Schedule K-1 (Form 1120S) 2013

This list identifies the codes used on Schedule K-1 for all shareholders and provides summarized reporting information for shareholders who file Form 1040. For detailed reporting and filing information, see the separate Shareholder's Instructions for Schedule K-1 and the instructions for your income tax return.

		Report on
1	**Ordinary business income (loss).** Determine whether the income (loss) is passive or nonpassive and enter on your return as follows:	
	Passive loss	See the Shareholder's Instructions
	Passive income	Schedule E, line 28, column (c)
	Nonpassive loss	Schedule E, line 28, column (h)
	Nonpassive income	Schedule E, line 28, column (j)
2	**Net rental real estate income (loss)**	See the Shareholder's Instructions
3	**Other net rental income (loss)**	
	Net income	Schedule E, line 28, column (g)
	Net loss	See the Shareholder's Instructions
4	**Interest income**	Form 1040, line 8a
5 a	**Ordinary dividends**	Form 1040, line 9a
5 b	**Qualified dividends**	Form 1040, line 9b
6	**Royalties**	Schedule E, line 4
7	**Net short-term capital gain (loss)**	Schedule D, line 5
8 a	**Net long-term capital gain (loss)**	Schedule D, line 12
8 b	**Collectibles (28%) gain (loss)**	28% Rate Gain Worksheet, line 4 (Schedule D instructions)
8 c	**Unrecaptured section 1250 gain**	See the Shareholder's Instructions
9	**Net section 1231 gain (loss)**	See the Shareholder's Instructions
10	**Other income (loss)**	
	Code	
	A Other portfolio income (loss)	See the Shareholder's Instructions
	B Involuntary conversions	See the Shareholder's Instructions
	C Sec. 1256 contracts and straddles	Form 6781, line 1
	D Mining exploration costs recapture	See Pub 535
	E Other income (loss)	See the Shareholder's Instructions
11	**Section 179 deduction**	See the Shareholder's Instructions
12	**Other deductions**	
	A Cash contributions (50%)	See the Shareholder's Instructions
	B Cash contributions (30%)	See the Shareholder's Instructions
	C Noncash contributions (50%)	See the Shareholder's Instructions
	D Noncash contributions (30%)	See the Shareholder's Instructions
	E Capital gain property to a 50% organization (30%)	See the Shareholder's Instructions
	F Capital gain property (20%)	See the Shareholder's Instructions
	G Contributions (100%)	See the Shareholder's Instructions
	H Investment interest expense	Form 4952, line 1
	I Deductions — royalty income	Schedule E, line 19
	J Section 59(e)(2) expenditures	See the Shareholder's Instructions
	K Deductions — portfolio (2% floor)	Schedule A, line 23
	L Deductions — portfolio (other)	Schedule A, line 28
	M Preproductive period expenses	See the Shareholder's Instructions
	N Commercial revitalization deduction from rental real estate activities	See Form 8582 instructions
	O Reforestation expense deduction	See the Shareholder's Instructions
	P Domestic production activities information	See Form 8903 instructions
	Q Qualified production activities income	Form 8903, line 7b
	R Employer's Form W-2 wages	Form 8903, line 17
	S Other deductions	See the Shareholder's Instructions
13	**Credits**	
	A Low-income housing credit (section 42(j)(5)) from pre-2008 buildings	See the Shareholder's Instructions
	B Low-income housing credit (other) from pre-2008 buildings	See the Shareholder's Instructions
	C Low-income housing credit (section 42(j)(5)) from post-2007 buildings	See the Shareholder's Instructions
	D Low-income housing credit (other) from post-2007 buildings	See the Shareholder's Instructions
	E Qualified rehabilitation expenditures (rental real estate)	See the Shareholder's Instructions
	F Other rental real estate credits	See the Shareholder's Instructions
	G Other rental credits	See the Shareholder's Instructions
	H Undistributed capital gains credit	Form 1040, line 71, box a
	I Biofuel producer credit	See the Shareholder's Instructions
	J Work opportunity credit	See the Shareholder's Instructions
	K Disabled access credit	See the Shareholder's Instructions
	L Empowerment zone employment credit	See the Shareholder's Instructions
	M Credit for increasing research activities	See the Shareholder's Instructions
	N Credit for employer social security and Medicare taxes	See the Shareholder's Instructions
	O Backup withholding	See the Shareholder's Instructions
	P Other credits	See the Shareholder's Instructions
14	**Foreign transactions**	
	A Name of country or U.S. possession	Form 1116, Part I
	B Gross income from all sources	Form 1116, Part I
	C Gross income sourced at shareholder level	Form 1116, Part I
	Foreign gross income sourced at corporate level	
	D Passive category	Form 1116, Part I
	E General category	Form 1116, Part I
	F Other	Form 1116, Part I
	Deductions allocated and apportioned at shareholder level	
	G Interest expense	Form 1116, Part I
	H Other	Form 1116, Part I
	Deductions allocated and apportioned at corporate level to foreign source income	
	I Passive category	Form 1116, Part I
	J General category	Form 1116, Part I
	K Other	Form 1116, Part I
	Other information	
	L Total foreign taxes paid	Form 1116, Part II
	M Total foreign taxes accrued	Form 1116, Part II
	N Reduction in taxes available for credit	Form 1116, line 12
	O Foreign trading gross receipts	Form 8873
	P Extraterritorial income exclusion	Form 8873
	Q Other foreign transactions	See the Shareholder's Instructions
15	**Alternative minimum tax (AMT) items**	
	A Post-1986 depreciation adjustment	See the Shareholder's Instructions and the Instructions for Form 6251
	B Adjusted gain or loss	See the Shareholder's Instructions and the Instructions for Form 6251
	C Depletion (other than oil & gas)	See the Shareholder's Instructions and the Instructions for Form 6251
	D Oil, gas, & geothermal — gross income	See the Shareholder's Instructions and the Instructions for Form 6251
	E Oil, gas, & geothermal — deductions	See the Shareholder's Instructions and the Instructions for Form 6251
	F Other AMT items	See the Shareholder's Instructions and the Instructions for Form 6251
16	**Items affecting shareholder basis**	
	A Tax-exempt interest income	Form 1040, line 8b
	B Other tax-exempt income	See the Shareholder's Instructions
	C Nondeductible expenses	See the Shareholder's Instructions
	D Distributions	See the Shareholder's Instructions
	E Repayment of loans from shareholders	See the Shareholder's Instructions
17	**Other information**	
	A Investment income	Form 4952, line 4a
	B Investment expenses	Form 4952, line 5
	C Qualified rehabilitation expenditures (other than rental real estate)	See the Shareholder's Instructions
	D Basis of energy property	See the Shareholder's Instructions
	E Recapture of low-income housing credit (section 42(j)(5))	Form 8611, line 8
	F Recapture of low-income housing credit (other)	Form 8611, line 8
	G Recapture of investment credit	See Form 4255
	H Recapture of other credits	See the Shareholder's Instructions
	I Look-back interest — completed long-term contracts	See Form 8697
	J Look-back interest — income forecast method	See Form 8866
	K Dispositions of property with section 179 deductions	See the Shareholder's Instructions
	L Recapture of section 179 deduction	See the Shareholder's Instructions
	M Section 453(l)(3) information	See the Shareholder's Instructions
	N Section 453A(c) information	See the Shareholder's Instructions
	O Section 1260(b) information	See the Shareholder's Instructions
	P Interest allocable to production expenditures	See the Shareholder's Instructions
	Q CCF nonqualified withdrawals	See the Shareholder's Instructions
	R Depletion information — oil and gas	See the Shareholder's Instructions
	S Amortization of reforestation costs	See the Shareholder's Instructions
	T Section 108(i) information	See the Shareholder's Instructions
	U Net investment income	See the Shareholder's Instructions
	V Other information	See the Shareholder's Instructions

Form **4562** | **Depreciation and Amortization** (Including Information on Listed Property) | OMB No. 1545-0172 **2013**

Department of the Treasury Internal Revenue Service (99) ► See separate instructions. ► Attach to your tax return. Attachment Sequence No. 179

Name(s) shown on return: INC | Identifying number: 26-4309504

Business or activity to which this form relates: FORM 1120S

Part I Election To Expense Certain Property Under Section 179
Note: *If you have any listed property, complete Part V before you complete Part I.*

1	Maximum amount (see instructions)	1	500,000.
2	Total cost of section 179 property placed in service (see instructions)	2	
3	Threshold cost of section 179 property before reduction in limitation (see instructions)	3	2,000,000.
4	Reduction in limitation. Subtract line 3 from line 2. If zero or less, enter -0-	4	
5	Dollar limitation for tax year. Subtract line 4 from line 1. If zero or less, enter -0-. If married filing separately, see instructions	5	

6	(a) Description of property	(b) Cost (business use only)	(c) Elected cost

7	Listed property. Enter the amount from line 29 ... 7		
8	Total elected cost of section 179 property. Add amounts in column (c), lines 6 and 7	8	
9	Tentative deduction. Enter the smaller of line 5 or line 8	9	
10	Carryover of disallowed deduction from line 13 of your 2012 Form 4562	10	
11	Business income limitation. Enter the smaller of business income (not less than zero) or line 5 (see instrs)	11	
12	Section 179 expense deduction. Add lines 9 and 10, but do not enter more than line 11	12	
13	Carryover of disallowed deduction to 2014. Add lines 9 and 10, less line 12 ► 13		

Note: *Do not use Part II or Part III below for listed property. Instead, use Part V.*

Part II Special Depreciation Allowance and Other Depreciation (Do not include listed property.) (See instructions.)

14	Special depreciation allowance for qualified property (other than listed property) placed in service during the tax year (see instructions)	14	5,012.
15	Property subject to section 168(f)(1) election	15	
16	Other depreciation (including ACRS)	16	

Part III MACRS Depreciation (Do not include listed property.) (See instructions.)

Section A

17	MACRS deductions for assets placed in service in tax years beginning before 2013	17	
18	If you are electing to group any assets placed in service during the tax year into one or more general asset accounts, check here ► ☐		

Section B – Assets Placed in Service During 2013 Tax Year Using the General Depreciation System

(a) Classification of property	(b) Month and year placed in service	(c) Basis for depreciation (business/investment use only — see instructions)	(d) Recovery period	(e) Convention	(f) Method	(g) Depreciation deduction
19a 3-year property						
b 5-year property						
c 7-year property		5,011.	7	HY	200DB	716.
d 10-year property						
e 15-year property						
f 20-year property						
g 25-year property			25 yrs		S/L	
h Residential rental property			27.5 yrs	MM	S/L	
			27.5 yrs	MM	S/L	
i Nonresidential real property			39 yrs	MM	S/L	
				MM	S/L	

Section C – Assets Placed in Service During 2013 Tax Year Using the Alternative Depreciation System

(a)	(b)	(c)	(d)	(e)	(f)	(g)
20a Class life					S/L	
b 12-year			12 yrs		S/L	
c 40-year			40 yrs	MM	S/L	

Part IV Summary (See instructions.)

21	Listed property. Enter amount from line 28	21	
22	Total. Add amounts from line 12, lines 14 through 17, lines 19 and 20 in column (g), and line 21. Enter here and on the appropriate lines of your return. Partnerships and S corporations — see instructions	22	5,728.
23	For assets shown above and placed in service during the current year, enter the portion of the basis attributable to section 263A costs ... 23		

2013	FEDERAL STATEMENTS	PAGE 1
	███ INC	███

STATEMENT 1
FORM 1120S, LINE 5
OTHER INCOME

VOIDED CHECKS	$	26.
RENTAL INCOME		6,000.
TOTAL	$	6,026.

STATEMENT 2
FORM 1120S, LINE 19
OTHER DEDUCTIONS

AUTO AND TRUCK EXPENSE	$	28,255.
BANK CHARGES		3,353.
COMMISSIONS		1,800.
CREDIT CARD FEES		5,304.
DELIVERY AND FREIGHT		12,022.
DUES AND SUBSCRIPTIONS		926.
EQUIPMENT RENTAL		2,163.
GIFTS		128.
INSURANCE		13,615.
LEGAL AND PROFESSIONAL		2,607.
OFFICE EXPENSE		5,255.
OUTSIDE SERVICES		11,692.
POSTAGE		556.
TELEPHONE		14,353.
TRADE SHOWS		2,789.
UTILITIES		3,028.
WEBSITE DESIGN		1,400.
TOTAL	$	109,246.

STATEMENT 3
FORM 1120S, SCHEDULE L, LINE 6
OTHER CURRENT ASSETS

	BEGINNING	ENDING
DUE FROM TAS	$ 72,245.	$ 75,675.
TOTAL	$ 72,245.	$ 75,675.

STATEMENT 4
FORM 1120S, SCHEDULE L, LINE 18
OTHER CURRENT LIABILITIES

	BEGINNING	ENDING
DUE TO OFFICER	$ 129,694.	$ 186,534.
PAYROLL TAXES PAYABLE	5,533.	1,589.
SALES TAX PAYABLE	2,852.	466.
TOTAL	$ 138,079.	$ 188,589.

INC

STATEMENT 5
FORM 1120S, SCHEDULE M-1, LINE 3
EXPENSES ON BOOKS NOT ON SCHEDULE K

PENALTIES	$	427.
TOTAL	$	427.

STATEMENT 6
FORM 1120S, SCHEDULE M-2, COLUMN A, LINE 5
OTHER REDUCTIONS

PENALTIES	$	427.
TOTAL	$	427.

STATEMENT 7
FORM 1125-A, LINE 5
OTHER COSTS

FREIGHT IN	$	5,013.
INSTALLATION EXPENSE		11,552.
SHIPPING SUPPLIES		659.
SHOP SUPPLIES		10,771.
TOTAL	$	27,995.

[REDACTED] INC [REDACTED]

COMPUTATION OF ENDING DEPRECIABLE ASSETS
FORM 1120S, SCHEDULE L, LINE 10A

BEGINNING DEPRECIABLE ASSETS	1,722.
DEPRECIABLE ASSETS PLACED IN SERVICE IN CURRENT YEAR	10,023.
DEPRECIABLE ASSETS SOLD DURING THE CURRENT YEAR	0.
ENDING BUILDINGS AND OTHER DEPRECIABLE ASSETS	11,745.

COMPUTATION OF ENDING ACCUMULATED DEPRECIATION
FORM 1120S, SCHEDULE L, LINE 10B

BEGINNING BALANCE OF ACCUMULATED DEPRECIATION	1,722.
CURRENT YEAR BOOK DEPRECIATION	5,728.
ACCUMULATED DEPRECIATION ON ASSETS SOLD THIS YEAR	0.
ENDING ACCUMULATED DEPRECIATION	7,450.

RECONCILIATION OF RETAINED EARNINGS
FORM 1120S, SCHEDULE L, LINE 24

BEGINNING RETAINED EARNINGS, SCH. L, LINE 24	67,157.
NET INCOME (LOSS) PER BOOKS (SCH. M-1, LINE 1)	9,309.
ENDING RETAINED EARNINGS, SCHEDULE L, LINE 24	76,466.

[REDACTED] INC [REDACTED]

SCHEDULE K, LINE 16C
NONDEDUCTIBLE EXPENSES

PENALTIES	$	427.
TOTAL	$	427.

2013 Shareholder's Basis Computation

S Corporation Name: [redacted] INC — Employer I.D. number: [redacted]

Name of Shareholder: [redacted] — Shareholder's I.D. number: [redacted]

1. STOCK BASIS AT BEGINNING OF TAX YEAR	67,157.

INCREASES:		DECREASES:	
2. Ordinary income	9,736.	13. Nondeductible expenses	427.
3. Net income from rental activities		14. Oil and gas depletion	
4. Net portfolio income		15. Ordinary loss	
5. Net gain under Section 1231		16. Net loss from rental activities	
6. Other income		17. Net portfolio loss	
7. Tax-exempt interest income		18. Net loss under Section 1231	
8. Other tax-exempt income		19. Other loss	
9. Net gain on disposition of Section 179 assets		20. Charitable contributions	
10. Oil and gas depletion in excess of basis		21. Section 179 expense deduction	
11. OTHER INCREASES:		22. Deductions related to portfolio income (loss)	
		23. Other deductions	
		24. Investment interest expense	
		25. Total foreign taxes	
		26. Section 59(e) expenses	
		27. Prior year loss in excess of basis	
		28. OTHER DECREASES:	
		29. Property distributions (including cash)	
12. TOTAL INCREASES: (add lines 2 - 11)	9,736.	30. TOTAL DECREASES (add lines 13 - 29)	427.

31. STOCK BASIS AT END OF TAX YEAR. (Line 1 plus line 12 minus line 30)	76,466.
32. DEBT BASIS AT BEGINNING OF TAX YEAR	0.
33. ADJUSTMENTS TO DEBT BASIS:	
34. DEBT BASIS AT END OF TAX YEAR (Combine Line 32 and 33)	0.
35. SHAREHOLDER'S TOTAL BASIS AT END OF TAX YEAR (Add Line 31 and 34)	76,466.

TAXABLE YEAR 2013 **California S Corporation Franchise or Income Tax Return** FORM **100S**

RP

3188496 13
TYB
INC

Schedule Q Questions: ***(continued on Side 2)***

A 1 FINAL RETURN? • ☐ Dissolved ☐ Surrendered (withdrawn) ☐ Merged/Reorganized ☐ IRC Section 338 sale ☐ QSub election

Enter date (mm/dd/yyyy) •

A 2 Is the S corporation deferring any income from the disposition of assets? • ☐ Yes ☐ No

If 'Yes' enter the year of disposition •

A 3 Is the S corporation reporting previously deferred income from: • ☐ Installment Sale • ☐ IRC § 1031 • ☐ IRC § 1033 • ☐ Other

STATE ADJUSTMENTS

	Line			
1	Ordinary income (loss) from trade or business activities from Schedule F (Form 100S, Side 4), line 22 or federal Form 1120S, line 21. If Schedule F (Form 100S, Side 4) was not completed, attach federal Form 1120S, page 1, and supporting schedules		1	9,736.
2	Foreign or domestic tax based on income or profits and California franchise or income tax deducted		2	800.
3	Interest on government obligations		3	
4	Net capital gain from Schedule D (100S), Section A & Section B. Attach Schedule D (100S). See instructions		4	
5	Depreciation and amortization adjustments. Attach Schedule B (100S)		5	3,978.
6	Portfolio income		6	
7	Other additions. Attach schedule(s)		7	
8	Total. Add line 1 through line 7		8	14,514.
9	Dividends received deduction. Attach Schedule H (100S)	9		
10	Water's-edge dividend deduction. Attach Schedule H (100S)	10		
11	Contributions. See instructions	11		
12	EZ or LAMBRA business expense and EZ net interest deduction	12		
13	Other deductions. Attach schedule(s)	13		
14	Total. Add line 9 through line 13		14	
15	Net income (loss) after state adjustments. Subtract line 14 from line 8		15	14,514.

INC 3188496

NET INCOME	16 Net income (loss) for state purposes. Use Schedule R if apportioning or allocating income ●	16	14,514.
	17 R&TC Section 23802(e) deduction. See instructions ● 17		
	18 Net operating loss deduction. See instructions ● 18		
	19 Pierce's disease, EZ, LARZ, TTA, or LAMBRA NOL deduction. See instructions ● 19		
	20 Disaster loss carryover deduction. See instructions ● 20		
	21 Net income for tax purposes. Combine line 17 through line 20. Subtract the result from line 16 ●	21	14,514.
TAXES	22 Tax. 1.5 % X line 21 (at least minimum franchise tax, if applicable). See instructions ●	22	800.
	23 New jobs credit a) amount generated ● b) amount claimed ●	23b	
	24a Credit name code ● amount ► 24a		
	24b Credit name code ● amount ► 24b		
	25 To claim more than two credits, see instructions ● 25		
	26 Add line 23b through line 25 ●	26	
	27 Balance. Subtract line 26 from line 22 (not less than minimum franchise tax plus QSub annual tax(es), if applicable) ●	27	800.
	28 Tax from Schedule D (100S). Attach Schedule D (100S). See instructions ●	28	
	29 Excess net passive income tax. See instructions ●	29	
	30 Total tax. Add line 27 through line 29 ●	30	800.
PAYMENTS	31 Overpayment from prior year allowed as a credit ● 31		
	32 2013 Estimated tax/QSub payments. See instructions ● 32 800.		
	33 2013 Withholding (Form 592-B and/or 593). See instructions ● 33		
	34 Amount paid with extension of time to file tax return ● 34		
	35 Total payments. Add line 31 through line 34 ●	35	800.
REFUND OR AMOUNT DUE	36 Franchise or income tax due. If line 30 is more than line 35, subtract line 35 from line 30. Go to line 39 ●	36	0.
	37 Overpayment. If line 35 is more than line 30, subtract line 30 from line 35 ●	37	
	38 Amount of line 37 to be credited to 2014 estimated tax ●	38	
	39 Use Tax. This is not a total line. See instructions ● 39		
	40 Refund. If the sum of line 38 and line 39 is less than 37, then subtract the result from line 37 ● See instructions to have the refund directly deposited. ☐ Checking ☐ Savings 40a ● Routing number 40b ● Type 40c ● Account number	40	
	41 a Penalties and interest. b ● ☐ Check if estimate penalty computed using Exception B or C. See instructions ●	41a	
	42 Total amount due. Add line 36, line 38, line 39, and line 41a, then subtract line 37 from the result ●	42	

Schedule Q Questions *(continued from Side 1)*

B 1 During this taxable year, did another person or legal entity acquire control or majority ownership (more than a 50% interest) of this corporation or any of its subsidiaries that owned California real property (i.e., land, buildings), leased such property for a term of 35 years or more, or leased such property from a government agency for any term? ● ☐ Yes ☒ No

2 During this taxable year, did this corporation or any of its subsidiaries acquire control or majority ownership (more than a 50% interest) in another legal entity that owned California real property (i.e., land, buildings), leased such property for a term of 35 years or more, or leased such property from a government agency for any term? ● ☐ Yes ☒ No

3 During this taxable year, has more than 50% of the voting stock of this corporation cumulatively transferred in one or more transactions after an interest in California real property (i.e., land buildings) was transferred to it that was excluded from property tax reassessment under Revenue and Taxation Code section 62(a)(2) and it was not reported on a previous year's tax return? ● ☐ Yes ☒ No (Yes required filing of statement, penalties may apply -- see instructions.)

Schedule Q Questions *(continued on Side 3)*

█████ INC 3188496

Schedule Q Questions *(continued from Side 2)*

C Principal business activity code. **Do not** leave blank ● 423800

Business activity SALES Product or service SERVICE

D Is this S corporation filing on a water's-edge basis pursuant to R&TC Sections 25110 and 25113 for the current taxable year? ● [ ] Yes [X] No

E Does this tax return include Qualified Subchapter S Subsidiaries? ● [ ] Yes [X] No

F Date incorporated (mm/dd/yyyy): 2/19/2009 Where: ● State CA Country USA

G Maximum number of shareholders in the S corporation at any time during the year. **Do not** leave blank ● 1

H Date business began in California or date income was first derived from California sources (mm/dd/yyyy): ● 12/31/2009

I Is the S corporation under audit by the IRS or has it been audited in a prior year? ● [ ] Yes [X] No

J Effective date of federal S election (mm/dd/yyyy): ● 2/13/2009

L Accounting method ● (1) [ ] Cash (2) [X] Accrual (3) [ ] Other

M Location of principal accounting records: ABOVE ADDRESS

N 'Doing business as' name. See instructions ●

O Have all required information returns (e.g., federal Form 1099, 8300 and state Forms 592, 592-B etc.) been filed with the Franchise Tax Board? [X] N/A [ ] Yes [ ] No

P Is this S corporation apportioning or allocating income to California using Schedule R? ● [ ] Yes [X] No

Q Has the S corporation included a reportable transaction or listed transaction within this return? See instructions for definitions ● [ ] Yes [X] No
If 'Yes,' complete and attach federal Form 8886, for each transaction.

R Did this S corporation file the federal Schedule M-3 (Form 1120S)? ● [ ] Yes [X] No

S Is form FTB 3544A, List of Assigned Credit Received and/or Claimed by an Assignee, attached to the return? ● [ ] Yes [ ] No

Schedule J Add-On Taxes and Recapture of Tax Credits. See instructions.

1	LIFO recapture due to S corporation election (IRC Section 1363(d) deferral: $) ●	1	
2	Interest computed under the look-back method for completed long-term contracts (attach form FTB 3834) ●	2	
3	Interest on tax attributable to installment: a) Sales of certain timeshares and residential lots ●	3a	
	b) Method for nondealer installment obligations ●	3b	
4	IRC Section 197(f)(9)(B)(ii) election ●	4	
5	Credit recapture name: ●	5	
6	Combine line 1 through line 5. Revise the amount on Side 2, line 36 or line 37, whichever applies, by this amount. Write 'Schedule J' to the left of line 36 or line 37 ●	6	

Sign Here

Under penalties of perjury, I declare that I have examined this return, including accompanying schedules and statements, and to the best of my knowledge and belief, it is true, correct, and complete. Declaration of preparer (other than taxpayer) is based on all information of which preparer has any knowledge.

Signature of officer ▶ Title: PRESIDENT & CEO Date: ● Telephone: 661-295-9330

Officer's email address (optional)

Paid Preparer's Use Only

Preparer's signature ▶ JOSH FARZAN, CPA Date: Check if self-employed ▶ [ ] ● PTIN: P01744958

Firm's name (or yours, if self-employed) and address ▶ FARZAN & FARZAN AAC, 19935 VENTURA BLVD SUITE. 302, WOODLAND HILLS, CA 91364 ● FEIN: 45-4629486 ● Telephone: (818) 381-5383

██ the FTB discuss this return with the preparer shown above? See instructions ● [X] Yes [ ] No

CASA0512L 02/05/14

INC 3188496

Schedule F Computation of Trade or Business Income. See instructions.

INCOME	1 a)	Gross receipts or sales 445,511. b) Less returns and allowances ______ c) Balance	1c	445,511.
	2	Cost of goods sold from Schedule V, line 8	2	159,172.
	3	Gross profit. Subtract line 2 from line 1c	3	286,339.
	4	Net gain (loss). Attach schedule	4	
	5	Other income (loss). Attach schedule SEE STATEMENT 1	5	6,026.
	6	**Total income (loss).** Combine line 3 through line 5	6	292,365.
DEDUCTIONS	7	Compensation of officers. Attach schedule. See instructions SEE STATEMENT 2	7	39,370.
	8	Salaries and wages	8	39,370.
	9	Repairs	9	4,077.
	10	Bad debts	10	
	11	Rents	11	57,038.
	12	Taxes	12	17,194.
	13	Interest	13	7,664.
	14a)	Depreciation 5,728. b) Less depreciation reported elsewhere ______ c) Balance	14c	5,728.
	15	Depletion	15	
	16	Advertising	16	1,838.
	17	Pension, profit-sharing plans, etc.	17	
	18	Employee benefit programs	18	1,104.
	19a)	Total travel and entertainment ______ b) Deductible amount	19b	
	20	Other deductions. Attach schedule SEE STATEMENT 3	20	109,246.
	21	**Total deductions.** Add line 7 through line 20	21	282,629.
	22	Ordinary income (loss) from trade or business. Subtract line 21 from line 6. Enter here and on Side 1, line 1	22	9,736.

The corporation ████ not be required to complete Schedule L and Schedule M-1. See Schedule L and Schedule M-1 instructions for reporting requirements.

Schedule L Balance Sheet

	Beginning of taxable year		End of taxable year	
Assets	(a)	(b)	(c)	(d)
1 Cash		2,227.		39,246.
2 a Trade notes and accounts receivable	181,223.		28,229.	
b Less allowance for bad debts		181,223.		28,229.
3 Inventories		163,262.		147,631.
4 Federal and state government obligations				
5 Other current assets. Attach sch(s) STMT 4		72,245.		75,675.
6 Loans to shareholders. Attach sch(s)				
7 Mortgage and real estate loans				
8 Other investments. Attach schedule(s)				
9 a Buildings and other fixed depreciable assets	1,722.		11,745.	
b Less accumulated depreciation	1,722.		7,450.	4,295.
10 a Depletable assets				
b Less accumulated depletion				
11 Land (net of any amortization)				
12 a Intangible assets (amortizable only)				
b Less accumulated amortization				
13 Other assets. Attach schedule(s)				
14 **Total assets**		418,957.		295,076.
Liabilities and shareholders' equity				
15 Accounts payable		141,526.		25,021.
16 Mortgages, notes, bonds payable in less than 1 year				
17 Other current liabilities. Att sch(s) STMT 5		138,079.		188,589.
18 Loans from shareholders. Attach sch(s)				
19 Mortgages, notes, bonds payable in 1 year or more		67,195.		
20 Other liabilities. Attach schedule(s)				
21 Capital stock		5,000.		5,000.
22 Paid-in or capital surplus				
23 Retained earnings		67,157.		76,466.
24 Adjustments. Attach schedule(s)				
25 Less cost of treasury stock				
26 **Total liabilities and shareholders' equity**		418,957.		295,076.

■ , INC 3188496

Schedule M-1 Reconciliation of Income (Loss) per Books With Income (Loss) per Return.

If the S corporation completed federal Schedule M-3 (Form 1120S). See instructions.

1 Net income per books	9,309.	5 Income recorded on books this year not included on Schedule K, line 1 through line 10b (itemize)	
2 Income included on Schedule K, line 1 through line 10b, not recorded on books this year (itemize)		a Tax-exempt interest $	
		b Other $	
		c Total. Add line 5a and line 5b	
3 Expenses recorded on books this year not included on Schedule K, line 1 through line 12e (itemize)		6 Deductions included on Schedule K, line 1 through line 12e, not charged against book income this year (itemize)	
a Depreciation $ 3,978.		a Depreciation $	
b State taxes $ 800.		b State tax refunds $	
c Travel & entertainment $		c Other $	
d Other STMT 6 $ 427.		d Total. Add line 6a through line 6c	
e Total. Add line 3a through line 3d	5,205.	7 Total. Add line 5c and line 6d	0.
4 Total. Add line 1 through line 3e	14,514.	8 Income (loss) (Schedule K, line 19, column d). Line 4 less line 7	14,514.

Schedule M-2 CA Accumulated Adjustments Account, Other Adjustments Account, and Other Retained Earnings. See instructions.

Important: Use California figures and federal procedures.	(a) Accumulated adjustments account	(b) Other adjustments account	(c) Other retained earnings (see instructions)
1 Balance at beginning of year	67,633.		
2 Ordinary income from Form 100S, Side 1, line 1	9,736.		
3 Other additions SEE STATEMENT 7	4,778.		
4 Loss from Form 100S, Side 1, line 1			
5 Other reductions SEE STATEMENT 8	(1,227)		
6 Combine line 1 through line 5	80,920.		
7 Distributions other than dividend distributions			
8 Balance at end of year. Subtract line 7 from line 6	80,920.		
9 Retained earnings at end of year. Add line 8, column (a) through column (c)			80,920.
☐ If the corporation has C corporation E&P at the end of the taxable year, check the box and enter the amount. See instructions			

Schedule V Cost of Goods Sold

1 Inventory at beginning of year	1	163,262.
2 Purchases	2	90,326.
3 Cost of labor	3	25,220.
4 Other IRC Section 263A costs. Attach schedule	4	
5 Other costs. Attach schedule STMT 9	5	27,995.
6 Total. Add line 1 through line 5	6	306,803.
7 Inventory at end of year	7	147,631.
8 Cost of goods sold. Subtract line 7 from line 6	8	159,172.

Was there any change in determining quantities, costs, or valuations between opening and closing inventory? ☐ Yes ☒ No

If 'Yes', attach an explanation. Enter California seller's permit number, if any ►

Method of inventory valuation COST

Check if the LIFO inventory method was adopted this taxable year for any goods. If checked, attach federal Form 970 ☐

If the LIFO inventory method was used for this taxable year, enter the amount of closing inventory computed under LIFO

██ ████, IN

Schedule K S Corporation Shareholder's Shares of Income, Deductions, Credits, etc.

	(a) Pro-rata share items		(b) Amount from federal K (1120S)	(c) California Adjustment	(d) Total amounts using California law
INCOME LOSS	1 Ordinary business income (loss)	1	9,736.	4,778.	14,514.
	2 Net rental real estate income (loss). Attach federal Form 8825	2			
	3a Other gross rental income (loss)	3a			
	b Expenses from other rental activities. Attach sch.	3b			
	c Other net rental income (loss). Subtract line 3b from line 3a	3c			
	4 Interest income	4			
	5 Dividends. See instructions	5			
	6 Royalties	6			
	7 Net short-term capital gain (loss). Attach Schedule D (100S)	7			
	8 Net long-term capital gain (loss). Attach Schedule D (100S)	8			
	9 Net Section 1231 gain (loss)	9			
OTHER INCOME LOSS	10a Other portfolio income (loss). Attach schedule	10a			
	b Other income (loss). Attach schedule	10b			
DEDUCTIONS	11 Expense deduction for recovery property (IRC Section 179 and R&TC Sections 17267.2 and 17268) Attach Schedule B (100S)	11			
	12a Charitable contributions	12a			
	b Investment interest expense	12b			
	c 1 Section 59(e)(2) expenditures	12c1			
	2 Type of expenditures	12c2			
	d Deductions — portfolio. Attach schedule	12d			
	e Other deductions. Attach schedule	12e			
CREDITS	13a Low-income housing credit. See instructions	13a			
	b Credits related to rental real estate activities. Attach schedule	13b			
	c Credits related to other rental activities. See instructions. Attach schedule	13c			
	d Other credits. Attach schedule	13d			
	e New jobs credit	13e			
	14 Total withholding allocated to all shareholders	14			
ALTERNATIVE MINIMUM TAX ITEMS	15a Depreciation adjustment on property placed in service after 12/31/86	15a			359.
	b Adjusted gain or loss. See instructions	15b			
	c Depletion (other than oil and gas)	15c			
	d 1 Gross income from oil, gas, and geothermal properties	15d1			
	2 Deductions allocable to oil, gas, and geothermal properties	15d2			
	e Other AMT items	15e			
ITEMS AFFECTING SHAREHOLDER BASIS	16a Tax-exempt interest income	16a			
	b Other tax-exempt income	16b			
	c Nondeductible expenses	16c	427.	800.	1,227.
	d Total property distributions (including cash) other than dividends distributions reported on line 17c	16d			
OTHER INFORMATION	17a Investment income. See instructions	17a			
	b Investment expenses. See instructions	17b			
	c Total dividend distributions paid from accumulated earnings and profits	17c			
	d Other items and amounts not included in lines 1-17b and lines 18a-e that are required to be reported separately to shareholders. Attach schedule ..... SEE STATEMENT 10	17d	SEE ATTACHED		SEE ATTACHED
OTHER STATE TAXES	18a Type of income	18a			
	b Name of state	18b			
	c Total gross income from sources outside CA. Attach sch.	18c			
	d Total applicable deductions and losses. Attach schedule	18d			
	e Total other state taxes. Check one: ☐ Paid ☐ Accrued	18e			
RECONCILIATION	19 Income (loss) (required only if Schedule M-1 must be completed). Combine line 1, line 2, and line 3c through line 10b. From the result, subtract the sum of lines 11, 12a, 12b, 12c1, 12d, and 12e	19	9,736.	4,778.	14,514.

TAXABLE YEAR **2013** FORM 100S, TRADE OR BUSINESS

S Corporation Depreciation and Amortization

CALIFORNIA SCHEDULE **B (100S)**

For use by S corporations only. Attach to Form 100S.

[redacted], INC — California corporation number 3188496

Part I Depreciation. Use additional sheets if necessary.

1 Enter federal depreciation from federal Form 4562, line 22. IRC Section 179 expense deduction is not included on this line. Get federal Form 4562 instructions. ..... 1 5,728.

California depreciation:

(a) Description of property	(b) Date acquired (mm/dd/yyyy)	(c) Cost or other basis	(d) Depreciation allowed or allowable in earlier years	(e) Method of figuring depreciation	(f) Life or rate	(g) Depreciation for this year
2 APPLE IPAD	9/13/2011	953.	477.	S/L	3	318.
LAPTOP COMPUTER	4/05/2012			200DB	5	0.
FURNITURE AND FIXTUR	1/31/2013	9,300.		200DB	7	1,329.
FURNITURE AND FIXTUR	7/09/2013	723.		200DB	7	103.

3 Add the amounts on line 2, column (g) ..... 3 1,750.

4 Subtract line 3 from line 1. If negative, use brackets. Enter here and on the applicable line of Form 100S, Side 6, Schedule K ..... 4 3,978.

5 Enter IRC Section 179 expense deduction here and on Form 100S, Side 1, line 13. Do not enter more than $25,000 ..... 5 0.

Part II Amortization. Use additional sheets if necessary.

1 Enter federal amortization from federal Form 4562, line 44 1

California amortization:

(a) Description of property	(b) Date acquired (mm/dd/yyyy)	(c) Cost or other basis	(d) Amortization allowed or allowable in earlier years	(e) R & TC section (See instr.)	(f) Period or percentage	(g) Amortization for this year
2						

3 Add the amounts on line 2, column (g) 3

4 California amortization adjustment. Subtract line 3 from line 1. If negative, use brackets. Enter here and on the applicable line of Form 100S, Side 6, Schedule K ..... 4 0.

Part III Depreciation and Amortization Adjustment

1 Combine the amounts on Part I, line 4, and Part II, line 4. Enter here (if negative, use brackets) and on Form 100S, Side 1, line 5. For passive activities, see instructions ..... 1 3,978.

TAXABLE YEAR 2013

Shareholder's Share of Income, Deductions, Credits, etc.

CALIFORNIA SCHEDULE **K-1 (100S)**

TYB 01-01-2013
6[redacted]

[redacted] INC

A Shareholder's percentage of stock ownership at year end ● 100 %

B Reportable transaction or tax shelter registration number(s):

C Check here if this is: ● (1) [ ] A final Schedule K-1 (2) [ ] An amended Schedule K-1

D What type of entity is this shareholder? ● (1) [X] Individual (2) [ ] Estate/Trust (3) [ ] Qualified Exempt Organization (4) [ ] Single Member LLC

E Is this shareholder a resident of California? ● [X] Yes ► [ ] No

Caution: Refer to the shareholder's instructions for Schedule K-1 (100S) before entering information from this schedule on your California tax return.

	(a) Pro-rata share items	(b) Amount from federal Schedule K-1 (1120S)	(c) California adjustment	(d) Total amounts using California law Combine (b) and (c) where applicable	(e) California source amounts and credits
INCOME/LOSS	1 Ordinary business income (loss)	9,736.	4,778.	● 14,514.	►
	2 Net rental real estate income (loss)			●	►
	3 Other net rental income (loss)			●	●
	4 Interest income			●	►
	5 Dividends. See instructions			●	►
	6 Royalties			●	►
	7 Net short-term capital gain (loss)			●	►
	8 Net long-term capital gain (loss)			●	►
	9 Net Section 1231 gain (loss)			●	►
OTHER INCOME OR LOSS	10a Other portfolio income (loss). Attach schedule			●	►
	b Other income (loss)			●	►

SHAREHOLDER 1

CASA0712L 01/21/14

INC

Caution: Refer to the shareholder's instructions for Schedule K-1 (100S) before entering information from this schedule on your California tax return.

	(a) Pro-rata share items	(b) Amount from federal Schedule K-1 (1120S)	(c) California adjustment	(d) Total amounts using California law Combine (b) and (c) where applicable	(e) California source amounts and credits
DEDUCTIONS	11 Expense deduction for recovery property (IRC Section 179 and R&TC Sections 17267.2 and 17268). Attach schedules				
	12a Charitable contributions				
	b Investment interest expense			•	►
	c 1 Section 59(e)(2) expenditures				
	2 Type of expenditures				
	d Deductions -- portfolio				
	e Other deductions				
CREDITS	13a Low-income housing credit. See instructions. Attach schedule			•	►
	b Credits related to rental real estate activities other than on line 13(a). Attach schedule			•	►
	c Credits related to other rental activities. See instructions. Attach sch			•	►
	d Other credits. Attach schedule			•	►
	e New jobs credit				
	14 Total withholding (equals amount on Form 592-B if calendar year)			•	►
ALTERNATIVE MINIMUM TAX AMT ITEMS	15a Depreciation adjustment on property placed in service after 12/31/86			359.	
	b Adjusted gain or loss				
	c Depletion (other than oil and gas)				
	d 1 Gross income from oil, gas, and geothermal properties				
	2 Deductions allocable to oil, gas, and geothermal properties				
	e Other AMT items. Attach schedule				
ITEMS AFFECTING SHAREHOLDERS BASIS	16a Tax-exempt interest income				
	b Other tax-exempt income				
	c Nondeductible expenses SEE ATT	427.	800.	1,227.	
	d Total property distributions (including cash) other than dividends distribution reported on line 17c			•	►
	e Repayment of loans from shareholders			•	►
OTHER INFO	17a Investment income. See instructions				
	b Investment expenses. See instructions				
	c Total taxable dividend distribution paid from accumulated earnings and profits. See instructions			•	►
	d Other information. See instructions	SEE ATTACHED		SEE ATTACHED	
OTHER STATE TAXES	18a Type of income				
	b Name of state				
	c Total gross income from sources outside California. Attach schedule				
	d Total applicable deductions and losses. Attach sch				
	e Total other state taxes. Check one: ☐ Paid ☐ Accrued			•	►

SHAREHOLDER 1 :

, INC

OTHER SHAREHOLDER INFORMATION

Table 1 -- Each shareholder's share of nonbusiness income from intangibles. See instructions.

Interest .... $ ______ Royalties .... $ ______ Dividends. $ ______

1231 Gains/Losses .... $ ______ Capital Gains/Losses .. $ ______ Other .... $ ______

FOR USE BY SHAREHOLDERS ONLY. SEE INSTRUCTIONS.

Table 2 -- Shareholder's pro-rata share of business income and factors -- See instructions.

A Shareholder's share of the S corporation's business income .... $ ______

B Shareholder's share of the nonbusiness income from real and tangible property sourced or allocable to California:

Capital Gains/Losses .... $ ______ Rents/Royalties .... $ ______

1231 Gains/Losses .... $ ______ Other .... $ ______

C Shareholder's share of the S corporation's property, payroll, and sales

Factors		Total within and outside California	Total within California
Property:	Beginning	$	$
	Ending	$	$
	Annual Rent Expense	$	$
Payroll		$	$
Sales		$	$

SHAREHOLDER 1 :

LINE 16C, COLUMN (D)
NONDEDUCTIBLE EXPENSES

PENALTIES	$	427.
STATE AND LOCAL TAXES BASED ON INCOME OR PROFITS		800.
TOTAL	$	1,227.

SUPPLEMENTAL INFORMATION

S CORPORATION'S AGGREGATE GROSS RECEIPTS	$	451,537.

[redacted] INC 3[redacted]

STATEMENT 1
FORM 100S, SCHEDULE F, LINE 5
OTHER INCOME

RENTAL INCOME	$	6,000.
VOIDED CHECKS		26.
	TOTAL $	6,026.

STATEMENT 2
FORM 100S, SCHEDULE F, LINE 7
COMPENSATION OF OFFICERS

NAME OF OFFICER	SOC. SEC. #	% OF TIME	% STOCK	COMPENSATION
[redacted]	[redacted]		100.000	39,370.
TOTAL COMPENSATION OF OFFICERS				39,370.
LESS: COMPENSATION CLAIMED ON SCHED. V AND ELSEWHERE				0.
OFFICERS' COMPENSATION DEDUCTED ON SCH. F (LINE 7)				39,370.

STATEMENT 3
FORM 100S, SCHEDULE F, LINE 20
OTHER DEDUCTIONS

AUTO AND TRUCK EXPENSE	$	28,255.
BANK CHARGES		3,353.
COMMISSIONS		1,800.
CREDIT CARD FEES		5,304.
DELIVERY AND FREIGHT		12,022.
DUES AND SUBSCRIPTIONS		926.
EQUIPMENT RENTAL		2,163.
GIFTS		128.
INSURANCE		13,615.
LEGAL AND PROFESSIONAL		2,607.
OFFICE EXPENSE		5,255.
OUTSIDE SERVICES		11,692.
POSTAGE		556.
TELEPHONE		14,353.
TRADE SHOWS		2,789.
UTILITIES		3,028.
WEBSITE DESIGN		1,400.
	TOTAL $	109,246.

STATEMENT 4
FORM 100S, SCHEDULE L, LINE 5
OTHER CURRENT ASSETS

	BEGINNING	ENDING
DUE FROM TAS	$ 72,245.	$ 75,675.
TOTAL	$ 72,245.	$ 75,675.

INC

STATEMENT 5
FORM 100S, SCHEDULE L, LINE 17
OTHER CURRENT LIABILITIES

	BEGINNING	ENDING
DUE TO OFFICER	$ 129,694.	$ 186,534.
PAYROLL TAXES PAYABLE	5,533.	1,589.
SALES TAX PAYABLE	2,852.	466.
TOTAL	$ 138,079.	$ 188,589.

STATEMENT 6
FORM 100S, SCHEDULE M-1, LINE 3
EXPENSES ON BOOKS NOT ON SCHEDULE K

PENALTIES	$ 427.
TOTAL	$ 427.

STATEMENT 7
FORM 100S, SCHEDULE M-2, LINE 3
OTHER ADDITIONS

CA DEPRECIATION ADJUSTMENT - ORDINARY INCOME	$ 3,978.
STATE AND LOCAL TAXES BASED ON INCOME OR PROFITS	800.
TOTAL	$ 4,778.

STATEMENT 8
FORM 100S, SCHEDULE M-2, LINE 5
OTHER REDUCTIONS

PENALTIES	$ 427.
STATE AND LOCAL TAXES BASED ON INCOME OR PROFITS	800.
TOTAL	$ 1,227.

STATEMENT 9
FORM 100S, SCHEDULE V, LINE 5
OTHER COSTS

FREIGHT IN	$ 5,013.
INSTALLATION EXPENSE	11,552.
SHIPPING SUPPLIES	659.
SHOP SUPPLIES	10,771.
TOTAL	$ 27,995.

STATEMENT 10
FORM 100S, SCHEDULE K, LINE 17D
OTHER ITEMS

S CORPORATION'S AGGREGATE GROSS RECEIPTS	$	451,537.

2013 California Shareholder's Basis Computation

S Corporation Name: [redacted] INC

Employer I.D. number: [redacted]

Name of Shareholder: [redacted]

Shareholder's I.D. number: [redacted]

1.	STOCK BASIS AT BEGINNING OF TAX YEAR	67,633.

INCREASES:		DECREASES:	
2. Ordinary income	14,514.	13. Nondeductible expenses	1,227.
3. Net income from rental activities		14. Oil and gas depletion	
4. Net portfolio income		15. Ordinary loss	
5. Net gain under Section 1231		16. Net loss from rental activities	
6. Other income		17. Net portfolio loss	
7. Tax-exempt interest income		18. Net loss under Section 1231	
8. Other tax-exempt income		19. Other loss	
9. Net gain on disposition of Section 179 assets		20. Charitable contributions	
10. Oil and gas depletion in excess of basis		21. Expense reduction for recovery property	
11. OTHER INCREASES:		22. Deductions related to portfolio income (loss)	
		23. Other deductions	
		24. Investment interest expense	
		25. Total other state taxes	
		26. Section 59(e) expenses	
		27. Prior year loss in excess of basis	
		28. OTHER DECREASES:	
		29. Property distributions (including cash)	
12. TOTAL INCREASES: (add lines 2 - 11)	14,514.	30. TOTAL DECREASES (add lines 13 - 29)	1,227.

31.	STOCK BASIS AT END OF TAX YEAR. (Line 1 plus line 12 minus line 30)	80,920.
32.	DEBT BASIS AT BEGINNING OF TAX YEAR	0.
33.	ADJUSTMENTS TO DEBT BASIS:	
34.	DEBT BASIS AT END OF TAX YEAR (Combine Line 32 and 33)	0.
35.	SHAREHOLDER'S TOTAL BASIS AT END OF TAX YEAR (Add Line 31 and 34)	80,920.

2014 INCOME TAX EXTENSION

Form **7004**
(Rev December 2012)
Department of the Treasury Internal Revenue Service

Application for Automatic Extension of Time To File Certain Business Income Tax, Information, and Other Returns

► File a separate application for each return.
► Information about Form 7004 and its separate instructions is at *www.irs.gov/form7004*.

Print or Type

Name: MAY NATIONAL, INC

Identifying number: [redacted]

Number, street, and room or suite number. (If P.O. box, see instructions.)

City or town, state, and ZIP code (If a foreign address, enter city, province or state, and country (follow the country's practice for entering postal code)).

Note. *File request for extension by the due date of the return for which the extension is granted. See instructions before completing this form.*

Part I — Automatic 5-Month Extension

1a Enter the form code for the return that this application is for (see below)

Application Is For:	Form Code	Application Is For:	Form Code
Form 1065	09	Form 1041 (estate other than a bankruptcy estate)	04
Form 8804	31	Form 1041 (trust)	05

Part II — Automatic 6-Month Extension

b Enter the form code for the return that this application is for (see below) 25

Application Is For:	Form Code	Application Is For:	Form Code
Form 706-GS(D)	01	Form 1120-ND (section 4951 taxes)	20
Form 706-GS(T)	02	Form 1120-PC	21
Form 1041 (bankruptcy estate only)	03	Form 1120-POL	22
Form 1041-N	06	Form 1120-REIT	23
Form 1041-QFT	07	Form 1120-RIC	24
Form 1042	08	Form 1120S	25
Form 1065-B	10	Form 1120-SF	26
Form 1066	11	Form 3520-A	27
Form 1120	12	Form 8612	28
Form 1120-C	34	Form 8613	29
Form 1120-F	15	Form 8725	30
Form 1120-FSC	16	Form 8831	32
Form 1120-H	17	Form 8876	33
Form 1120-L	18	Form 8924	35
Form 1120-ND	19	Form 8928	36

2 If the organization is a foreign corporation that does not have an office or place of business in the United States, check here ► ☐

3 If the organization is a corporation and is the common parent of a group that intends to file a consolidated return, check here ► ☐
If checked, attach a statement, listing the name, address, and Employer Identification Number (EIN) for each member covered by this application.

Part III — All Filers Must Complete This Part

4 If the organization is a corporation or partnership that qualifies under Regulations section 1.6081-5, check here ► ☐

5a The application is for calendar year 20 14, or tax year beginning ________, 20 __, and ending ________, 20 __

b **Short tax year.** If this tax year is less than 12 months, check the reason: ☐ Initial return ☐ Final return
☐ Change in accounting period ☐ Consolidated return to be filed ☐ Other (see instructions – attach explanation)

6	Tentative total tax	6	0.
7	**Total** payments and credits (see instructions)	7	0.
8	**Balance due.** Subtract line 7 from line 6 (see instructions)	8	0.